Mastering Money

Life Skills Lab

Good Buddy Books

A Hands-On Guide to Managing Money, Beating Debt, and Building Wealth

Table of Contents

Life Skills Lab Foreword

Money can be a mystery, especially when you're just starting out.

You see adults working hard, paying bills, talking about debt, saving for retirement, and maybe even stressing over the cost of things like rent or groceries. But where does all that money actually go? And more importantly, how can you make sure your money works for you instead of the other way around?

That's what *Mastering Money* is all about.

This book was written to help you understand what most adults wish they'd learned much earlier: how to earn money, manage it wisely, and use it to build a life that feels stable and free. You don't need to be an accountant or an investor to be good with money; you just need to understand the basics, stay consistent, and make smart decisions.

Inside, you'll find relatable stories, clear explanations, and hands-on activities that makes managing money make sense. You'll learn how paychecks work, what a budget really is, how interest and credit can be your friend or your enemy, and how even small savings can grow into big goals over time.

About the Life Skills Lab Series

Mastering Money is part of the **Life Skills Lab** series; a growing collection of workbooks designed to teach the real-world lessons that so many adults say they never got in school. From giving and gratitude to entrepreneurship, budgeting, critical thinking, and communication, each title in the series explores essential skills that help young people grow into capable, confident adults.

These books are written by a husband-and-wife team with their own children in mind; lessons we want our kids to learn so they can thrive as they grow up and become even more successful than we are. We believe that understanding how to manage money, give generously, and think independently are some of the most valuable skills a person can develop.

Mastering Money is one of the most in-depth books in the series, covering earning, budgeting, saving, debt, and investing. Current and future **Life Skills Lab** titles will expand on these ideas, diving deeper into entrepreneurship, smart shopping, media literacy, giving back, and other life skills that empower both kids and families to live wisely and well.

Whether you're reading this on your own, learning alongside your parents, or using it in a homeschool or classroom setting, remember: this book is more than information; it's a toolkit for your future.

Money doesn't have to be confusing or stressful. Once you understand how it flows, how to guide it, and how to use it to build your goals, you'll realize that financial freedom isn't about luck or talent, it's about knowledge and discipline.

So, grab a pencil, open your mind, and get ready to think like a financial scientist.

Part 1: Understanding Money

Chapter 1: Why Personal Finance Matters

Opening Story: Jordan's Tablet Plan

Jordan had been sketching in the margins of his notebook for months, making little comic panels and logo ideas that looked surprisingly professional. His older cousin visited one weekend and showed Jordan how a tablet with a pressure-sensitive stylus could turn those sketches into real digital art. The device was thin and bright; the pen glided like ice. The price tag: **$650** plus a protective case and a drawing app.

At first, Jordan felt the distance between his idea and that price like a canyon. He had **$242** saved from birthdays and mowing a few lawns. But then he did something important: he didn't give up; he **did the math**. If he set aside $30 each week (allowance plus odd jobs) he could reach his goal by the end of the year, sooner if he picked up extra work in the summer. The number still felt big, but the path no longer felt mysterious.

A few days later, Jordan's friend Leo told him he was getting a different tablet **right away**. Leo's family planned to buy it on a store card and "pay it off later." Leo's would show up next week, while Jordan would be waiting months. That stung a little…until Jordan's dad sat down with him and explained how credit works.

"If we pay over time and don't pay in full each month," his dad said, "the final price isn't $650 anymore. Interest turns $650 into something like $700 or $800, sometimes more depending on how long it takes and the interest rate." Leo might be unboxing faster, but he was also agreeing to a **higher** price.

Jordan decided he liked his plan better; **no debt, no stress**, and a tablet that would feel earned. He set up jars: *Tablet*, *Giving*, *Everyday*, and *Savings*. He wrote down his weekly goal and taped it to the wall. Within two weeks he'd found a neighbor who needed help organizing their garage. Within a month he was closer to the goal than he'd expected, and much more confident. His plan wasn't flashy. It was **steady**, and it was working.

What Is Personal Finance?

Personal finance is **everything you do with money**: how you **earn** it, **spend** it, **save** it, **invest** it, and **give** it. It includes everyday choices (whether to buy something now or later) and big decisions (how much to set aside for emergencies or how to prepare for college and careers). When people say "get better with money," they usually mean, "build habits that let your money support your life, values, and future."

Think of personal finance as a **system of small, repeatable moves**. If you decide every dollar should have a job, you begin to plan your dollars instead of wondering where they went. If you make saving automatic, you grow a cushion without needing daily willpower. If you compare prices and avoid impulse buys, you keep more of what you earn. These simple moves add up.

Personal finance is also **not** just for adults. Kids and teens manage money too; allowances, gifts, earnings from chores or small jobs, fundraiser money, and birthday windfalls. Learning how to plan your money now builds confidence that lasts. The goal isn't to become a mini-accountant. It's to understand **how money flows** so you can guide that flow on purpose.

Another key idea: personal finance is **personal**. Two families with the same income can make very different choices because their priorities differ. One might prioritize travel; another might prioritize paying off debt or building a home library. A "right" answer is the one that matches your values **and** keeps you safe from avoidable financial stress.

Finally, personal finance is not a one-time project; it's a **practice**. You'll adjust as life changes (new goals, new jobs, new needs), but the core skills (deciding, planning, checking in) stay the same. Learn the system once; keep applying it forever.

Reflection Question:

- When you think about money, which part feels strongest for you right now: Earning, spending, saving, investing, or giving? Which part feels like it needs more attention?

Personal Finance is Simple, but not Easy

The basic formula of personal finance can fit on a sticky note:

Spend less than you earn. Save and invest the difference. Repeat.

If it's that simple, why does it feel so hard? Because money isn't only about math; it's about **behavior** and **feelings**. We buy to celebrate or to feel better. Ads push us toward "must-have" upgrades. Friends post their highlight reels. A sale timer counts down and nudges us to act fast. And sometimes, we just haven't seen a better way modeled at home or school.

"Not easy" doesn't mean "not possible." It means we need **guardrails**. Guardrails are small designs that make the right choice the easy choice. A few powerful ones:

- **Automate saving.** Move money to savings the day you get paid, so you never feel like you "lost" it.
- **Name your dollars.** Give every dollar a job (rent, groceries, bus pass, savings, charity) so "extra" money doesn't vanish.
- **Use waiting rules.** Want something non-essential? Wait 24 hours (or a week for big items). Most impulse desires fade.
- **Set spending triggers.** If a purchase is over $X, you review it with a parent or partner first. More eyes, smarter choices.

Another reason it's hard: we often **confuse wants and needs** or underestimate "small leaks" like subscriptions or snacks out. Ten dollars here and there can add up to hundreds each month. The "simple but not easy" truth pushes us to slow down and ask: *Is this the best use of my next dollar?*

Parents: you can model this in little ways, like saying out loud, "We're choosing pasta night at home so we can save for the weekend museum trip," or, "We'll wait three days; if we still want it, we'll budget for it." Kids notice the calm that planning brings.

Reflection Question:

- Which guardrail would help you most this month: automation, naming dollars, waiting rules, or spending triggers?

The State of Money in America

Why learn this now? Because a lot of adults are **struggling**, and you can learn from their experience. Recent surveys show **many Americans live paycheck to paycheck**, which means most of their income is gone by month's end. One widely cited 2025 report (PNC's 2025 Financial Wellness Data) put that share at **about two-thirds (67%)**, up from 2024.

Savings are also thin for many households. The Federal Reserve's *Survey of Household Economics and Decision-Making* shows just over half of adults report having at least three months of emergency savings (a level the Fed tracks annually). Other research finds that roughly one in four Americans have no emergency savings at all, and many would turn to a credit card to cover a $1,000 surprise.

Credit cards, when used with great discipline and paid in full monthly, can be helpful tools. When balances carry over, they become expensive and can derail your financial growth. In 2025, typical credit card Annual Percentage Rates (APRs; the total annual cost of a loan or credit, including interest and fees) are around the **low-to-mid-20%** range, according to Federal Reserve data and industry trackers. That means a $1,000 balance spread out over a year will cost over $120 in interest in addition to the $1,000 owed.

As for balances, the New York Fed reported credit card debt totaling about **$1.21 trillion** in Q2 2025 (an increase from the prior quarter) while several analyses put the **average balance per person** with unpaid card debt in the **$6,700–$7,300** range (it varies by source and method).

What do these numbers mean for you? They show why **habits matter** more than ever. People don't wake up one day with perfect finances; they build them inch by inch. If you start with clear plans (budgeting, saving first, avoiding high-interest debt) you avoid the traps that statistics describe. And if you're already an adult reading this with a child, take heart: habits can change at any age. One small, consistent change beats a giant plan you don't follow.

Reflection Question:

- Which statistic hits you hardest: paycheck-to-paycheck, emergency savings, or credit card interest? Why?

Why Learning Early Matters

Starting early multiplies your advantage. Habits compound just like money does. If a 12-year-old saves $20 a month for a year, they don't just have $240; they have a **system** (a plan, a rhythm, a sense of control) that's rare even among adults. That system scales when the numbers get bigger.

Starting early also **reduces costly mistakes** later. When you learn the difference between a debit card and a credit card now, you won't be surprised by interest later. When you understand how a budget tells your money what to do, you won't feel confused at the end of the month. When you practice saving for a goal like Jordan's tablet, you learn the patience that powers bigger goals, such as cars, college, or a business.

There's another benefit: **confidence**. Money confusion creates stress; money understanding creates calm. Kids who learn how to handle money become teens who ask smarter questions at their first job, who know how to set up direct deposit, who can avoid predatory loans, and who can begin saving and investing towards larger goals.

Parents sometimes worry, "Won't talking about money make kids anxious?" In our experience, **silence creates more anxiety**. Honest, hopeful conversations paired with small actions kids can take replaces mystery with understanding. The goal isn't to talk about money all the time; it's to build enough clarity that money becomes **just one more thing you're good at**.

Finally, starting early allows you to **connect money to values**. You can decide not just what you're saving for, but **why**. You can plan to give some of your money away, even when amounts are small, so generosity grows alongside your bank balance.

Reflection Question:

- What money lesson has made the biggest impact on you to date?

The Power of Financial Confidence

Financial confidence doesn't mean you're rich; it means you have a **plan**. You know what's coming in, what's going out, and why. You know how much cushion you have for surprises, and you know how to adjust. That calm changes the way families feel at home. It changes how kids and teens feel at school and work. It turns big-ticket items from panic into planning.

Confidence shows up in everyday ways:

- You can look at a price and decide if it fits your **plan**, not just your mood.
- You know what to do when your bike needs a repair or the family car needs tires.
- You can say "not yet" to an impulse and "yes" to a goal.
- You feel **proud** to give, because you planned for it.

Confidence also grows through **tiny wins**. Setting aside $5 this week is a win. Checking your balance before you spend is a win. Saying "let's wait 24 hours" is a win. These wins build trust in yourself: *I follow through.* Money becomes less about fear and more about choice.

Parents can fan this flame by celebrating effort: "I noticed you checked the price per ounce," or "Thanks for reminding us to compare plans before we subscribed." Praise the **process**, not just the result. Process is what kids can repeat.

Reflection Question:

- Picture a financially confident version of you. What is that person doing differently in a normal week?

Pulling It Together

If you remember one thing from this chapter, let it be this: **personal finance is a set of learnable skills.** You don't need to be "good at math" to be good with money. You need a few simple tools and the willingness to practice. In this book, you'll learn how people earn money (as employees, business owners, and investors), how to manage money with a budget and smart spending, how to build savings, how to understand debt (and get out of it), and how to make investing work for you over time.

You'll also see how **giving** fits into a healthy money life. Generosity isn't separate from financial wisdom; it's part of it. When you plan to give, you practice gratitude, reduce fear, and remember that money is a tool to **serve people**, not the other way around.

Jordan's tablet didn't arrive overnight. But when it did, it came with something better than a box to open: it came with the knowledge that he could **set a goal, build a plan, and stick to it**. That's the real gift of learning personal finance: not just getting things you want, but becoming someone who can **trust themselves** to reach important goals.

Chapter 1 Reflection Questions:

- What do you want money to do **for** you and your family (in the next month, year, and five years)?
- Which guardrail (automation, naming dollars, waiting rules, spending triggers) would help you most this month?
- Which "State of Money" stat surprised you the most, and what small habit could you start to avoid that trap?
- What money habit would future-you thank you for starting **today**?

Activities: Why Personal Finance Matters

1) Money Snapshot

List your typical weekly or monthly **money in** (allowance, gifts, small jobs). Then, list your typical **money out** (snacks, apps, activities, giving).

Circle one category to **shrink by $5–$10** this week and one category to **grow** (like savings or giving).

Source of Money In	Weekly	Monthly
	$	$
	$	$
	$	$

Source of Money Out	Weekly	Monthly
	$	$
	$	$
	$	$
Giving	$	$
Saving	$	$

2) Build a Guardrail

Choose one guardrail to install this week:

- Set up **automatic savings** (even $5).
- **Name your dollars** for next week (what job does each dollar have?).
- Use a **24-hour rule** for non-essentials.

- Pick a **review threshold** (talk together before spending more than $X).

Write one sentence about how it felt and what you learned.

____

____

____

3) Talk to an Adult

Ask a parent, guardian, or mentor:

- "What's a money decision you wish you'd made earlier?"
- "What's a money habit you're proud of?"

Write down the most helpful advice you heard and one action you'll take because of it.

____

____

____

____

____

____

____

____

____

Chapter 2: The Language of Money

Opening Story: "Where Did It All Go?"

Every Saturday morning, Maya checked her wallet and sighed. She was supposed to have twenty dollars left from last week's allowance and babysitting money. Instead, there were six. She couldn't even remember where it had gone. A drink at the corner store? A few online game add-ons? Snacks after school? Nothing huge, just lots of little somethings.

That afternoon, she sat down at the kitchen table with her mom, who was balancing the family budget. "I feel like my money just disappears," Maya said. Her mom smiled. "It doesn't disappear," she said. "It moves. You just haven't learned to *see* it yet."

Together they started listing where Maya's money flowed in and out. She earned money from babysitting and allowance. She spent money on small treats and digital downloads. She had savings for a new backpack. Her mom drew arrows between them; money *in*, money *out*, and money *set aside*. Suddenly, it didn't feel like magic, it felt like a *map*.

By the end of the day, Maya wasn't just wondering where her money went, she was tracking it. "It's like learning a new language," her mom said. "Once you speak it, you can start directing where the words go."

The Big Five Words

If you can learn these five words, you can understand almost every money conversation you'll ever have:

1. Income: the money that *comes in.*
It can come from work, allowance, gifts, or even your money earning more money (like interest from a savings account). Adults earn income through jobs, business profits, and investments.

2. Expenses: the money that *goes out.*
These are things you pay for: food, gas, clothes, subscriptions, bills. For kids and teens, it might be snacks, games, or sports gear. Some expenses are necessary (like groceries or school supplies). Others are optional (like fast food or extra clothes).

3. Assets: the things you *own* that have value.
A savings account, a car, a house, and even a bike can be assets. They're things that can help you or that could be sold for money later.

4. Liabilities: the things you *owe.*
If you borrow money, you have a liability. That could be a student loan, a car loan, or even a balance on a credit card. Liabilities take money *out* of your future income.

5. Net Worth: what's *left* after you subtract what you owe from what you own.
It's like taking inventory of your financial life. If your assets are worth

$5,000 and your liabilities total $1,500, your net worth is $3,500. It's not about bragging, it's about seeing whether you're moving in the right direction over time.

Even adults who earn good incomes can have a low net worth if their debts grow faster than their savings. On the flip side, a teen who saves consistently might already have positive net worth. Every smart decision adds up.

Reflection Question:

- Which of these big five words feels most familiar to you, and which one do you want to understand better?

Cash Flow in Action

Money is always moving. It's not something that just sits still in a wallet or bank. Every dollar you earn has a *journey*.

Imagine a stream flowing through your life:

- At the top of the stream is **income**, the water pouring in.
- Along the sides are **expenses**, like buckets dipping into the stream.
- What's left moves into **savings**, a calm pool building up.
- From there, some flows into **investing**, where it can grow.
- Finally, some is redirected toward **giving**, where it flows into someone else's life.

If too many buckets dip in at once, your stream runs dry. But if you build barriers (like budgeting and planning), you can keep water in the stream and even help it grow.

For example:

- If you earn $25 per week and spend $18, you have $7 left to direct elsewhere. Maybe $5 to save and $2 to give.
- If you keep this pattern up weekly, you'd have over $100 saved in less than five months.

Parents can model this too: show kids how their income covers essentials (housing, food, transportation), then point out how saving and giving fit into the same picture. Seeing money as flow helps kids (and adults) stop wondering *"where it went"* and start deciding *"where it should go."*

Reflection Question:

- If your money were a stream, where would most of your water be flowing right now?

Interest, Inflation, and Compound Growth

Money has a secret power: it can *grow* or *shrink* depending on what you do with it. Three ideas control that growth:

Interest

Interest is the cost of using money, or the reward for lending it.

- When you **borrow**, you pay interest.
- When you **save or invest**, you earn interest.

If you put $100 in a savings account that pays 3% annual interest, you'll earn $3 after one year. Not exciting? Think again, because now your balance is $103, and *next year* you'll earn interest on all of it.

Compound Growth

That's where the magic happens. Compound interest means you earn interest *on the interest you already earned.* Over time, this snowballs.

If you save $100 a month from age 12 to 22 and earn an average of 7% per year, you'll have around $17,000. But if you wait until 22 and start saving $200 a month until 27, you'll only have around $14,000, even though you saved the same total amount ($12,000)! Time multiplies your results.

That's why people say, "Time is your best investment partner." The earlier you start, the easier it gets.

Inflation

But there's a villain in the story: inflation.
In the context of personal finance, inflation is when prices rise over time, meaning your money buys less. If a candy bar costs $1 today and $1.10 next year, that's 10% inflation. It doesn't sound like much, but over 10–20 years, inflation can quietly eat away at savings if they're not growing fast enough.

The goal is simple: make your money *grow faster* than prices rise.

Reflection Question:

Would you rather have $100 today or $110 five years from now? Why? What role does compound growth and inflation play in your decision?

Visualizing the Growth

It's easier to *see* how money grows than just read about it.
Imagine three jars sitting side by side, each starting with $100.

- **Jar 1: No Growth (Hidden Under the Bed)**
  Ten years later, it's still $100. Safe, but it hasn't grown, and inflation means it actually buys *less*.
- **Jar 2: Simple Growth (Saving)**
  You earn $3 each year in interest. After 10 years, it's $130. Nice, but you only earned on the original $100.
- **Jar 3: Compound Growth (Investing)**
  You earn 3% interest *on everything in the jar.* After 10 years, it's $134; not much more at first, but over 30 years it becomes about $242 (vs. $190 for simple growth after 30 years). Time doubles the result.

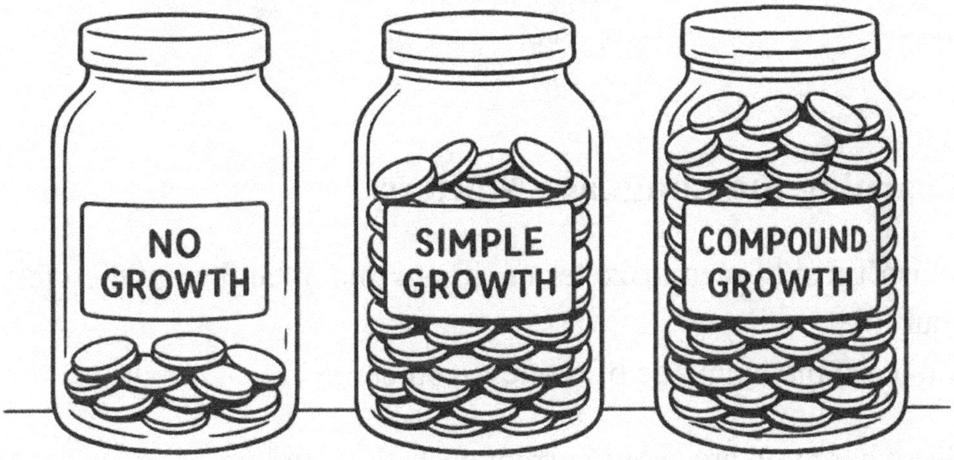

The earlier you start and the longer you stay invested, the more time works for you.

Parents can show this concept visually with a simple graph or a free compound-interest calculator online. Watching the curve bend upward slowly at first, then steep over time is one of the most powerful "aha" moments in all of finance.

Below is an example of a 12 year old who puts $100 into an investment account and adds $25 per month until they are 18 years old. In this example, they earn 7% per year, a realistic amount for a total market index fund.

By the end of this 6 year period, their $1,900 invested will have grown to $2,364, a gain of over 20%! Had they put the money in a jar under their bed instead, the total at the end of six years would be $464 lower.

Year	Deposit	Interest	Ending balance
1	$400.00	$16.51	$416.51
2	$300.00	$38.66	$755.17
3	$300.00	$62.37	$1,117.54
4	$300.00	$87.74	$1,505.27
5	$300.00	$114.88	$1,920.15
6	$300.00	$143.92	$2,364.07

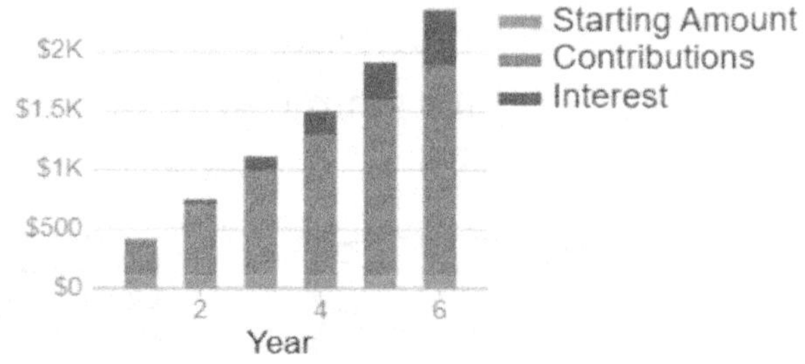

Why Learning the Language Matters

The goal isn't just to memorize terms, it's to understand what they tell you about your life.
Once you learn the language of money, you can:

- See where you are (your current cash flow and net worth).
- Plan where you want to go (your goals).

- Measure how you're doing (your progress).

Think of it like learning to read a map. Once you can read the symbols, you're not lost anymore; you're navigating.

Money is everywhere, but confidence with it is rare. People who can "speak" money have options. They can understand paychecks, compare job offers, choose better savings accounts, avoid bad loans, and make smart purchases.

The more fluent you become, the more you'll notice: money conversations stop feeling scary. They become *strategy sessions.*

Reflection Question:

- What's one money "word" that used to sound confusing but makes more sense now?

Chapter 2 Reflection Questions:

1. Which of the big five money words (income, expenses, assets, liabilities, net worth) feels most relevant to you right now?
2. What's something in your life that adds value (an asset) and something that costs you over time (a liability)?
3. How does compound growth motivate you to start early?

Activities: The Language of Money

1. Follow Your Money

Track your money for seven days. Write down everything you earn or receive (income). Write down everything you spend (expenses). At the end of the week, add them up.

How much money flowed in?

____

____

How much money flowed out?

____

____

What's left to save or give?

____

____

2. Build Your Mini Balance Sheet

Fill in the two columns below. Assets include savings and valuable items that you own. Liabilities are debts that you owe. Use the space in the table to calculate each if needed.

Subtract Assets – Liabilities to find your net worth.

Even if it's small or zero, you've just created your first financial statement!

What I Own (Assets)	What I Owe (Liabilities)	Net Worth
Total Assets: **$** -	**Total Liabilities:** **$** =	**Net Worth:** **$**

3. Vocabulary Match-Up

Match each word to a real-life example from your life or home.

Income = ____

Expense = ____

Asset = ____

Liability = ____

Discuss your answers with a parent or friend.

Part 2: Earning Money

Chapter 3: How People Make Money

Opening Story: The $100 Challenge

When Liam's class started a "Money Makers Week," everyone had to come up with a way to earn their first $100. Some kids mowed lawns, some sold friendship bracelets, and one student made a short online tutorial for drawing animals. Liam wasn't sure what to do at first, so he asked his dad for ideas.

"People make money in three main ways," his dad said. "They work for it, they build something that earns it, or they invest in something that grows it."

That week, Liam decided to test all three. He washed cars for neighbors (employee). He designed and sold pet name tags with a 3D printer (business owner). And with the few dollars left over, he helped his dad buy shares in a company that made sports gear (investor).

By the end of the week, Liam didn't just earn money; he discovered that money can come from **different directions** depending on how you use your time, creativity, and patience.

The Three Main Ways People Earn Money

1. Employee: Trading Time for Wages

This is the most common way people earn money: they **work for someone else**.

When you're an employee, you trade your time, energy, and skills for a paycheck. You agree to certain hours or tasks, and in return, you get paid a set amount (hourly or salary).

For adults, this might mean working as a teacher, engineer, nurse, or store manager. For teens, it might mean babysitting, tutoring, or working at a local shop. Even doing chores for an allowance is a simple example, as work is exchanged for payment.

Pros:

- Predictable income
- Structure and stability
- Often includes benefits like insurance or paid time off

Cons:

- Limited control: someone else decides your pay and hours

- Hard to scale: you can't work 100 hours a day
- Income stops if you stop working

Still, being a good employee is one of the most valuable skills you can build. It teaches responsibility, teamwork, and how to deliver results. Many entrepreneurs start as employees to learn the ropes.

Reflection Question:

- What kind of job do you think you'd be best at right now if you had to earn $100 this week?

2. Business Owner: Building Something That Earns Money

Rather than working for someone else, business owners, or **entrepreneurs**, build something of their own that provides value to others. That might be a product, a service, or a mix of both.

An entrepreneur could own a landscaping company, open a coffee shop, or sell digital art online. The idea is to solve a problem or make life easier or more enjoyable for others. If they do it well customers pay for that value, and the business earns income even when the owner isn't personally doing every task.

For kids and teens, this might look like:

- Running a **lemonade stand** or snack booth at a sports event
- Starting a **pet-sitting or dog-walking** service
- Selling **handmade crafts or art prints** online
- Buying and reselling **underappreciated items** from garage sales and thrift stores.
- Offering **tutoring or tech help** to younger students or seniors

Pros:

- Unlimited potential: your income can grow as your ideas do
- You're your own boss
- You create jobs or opportunities for others

Cons:

- Risk: not every idea works
- Irregular income
- It is common to lose money for a while before you become profitable.
- A lot of responsibility

Entrepreneurs are problem-solvers. They see needs and fill them. Sometimes they fail, but they learn faster than most people because they try new things constantly.

Reflection Question:

- Think of something that annoys people or could be made easier. How might you turn that into a business idea?

3. Investor: Making Money Work for You

Investors use money to earn **more money**. Instead of trading hours, they use capital (money or assets) to buy something that grows in value or produces income. Common examples are:

- **Stocks**: buying ownership in a company
- **Bonds**: lending money to companies or governments in exchange for interest
- **Real estate**: owning property that increases in value or collects rent
- **Small businesses**: investing in an idea or helping someone else start a business.

For kids, investing might look like:

- Buying a few shares in a company they know (through a parent or youth investing app)
- Starting a **high yield savings account (HYSA)** and watching interest grow
- Helping fund a school project that sells something and shares profits

Pros:

- Money grows without trading time
- Compound growth over years can multiply returns

- Offers financial freedom later in life

Cons:

- Takes time and patience
- Risk of loss (investments can go down)
- Requires learning and discipline
- It's hard to make a lot of money if you don't have a lot to invest

Investors understand one simple truth: the earlier you start, the more time your money has to grow. Even small investments can snowball with consistency.

Reflection Question:

- If you could invest in any business or idea you believe in, what would it be, and why?

Scaling: Why Some Income Grows Faster

Not all income grows at the same speed.

- **Employees** trade hours for money, meaning income rises slowly unless they get raises or promotions.
- **Business owners** can scale because they sell to many customers, not just one boss.
- **Investors** can scale because money grows while they sleep.

It's like three different tools for earning:

- The **shovel** (employee): reliable but one dig at a time.
- The **machine** (business): multiplies what one person can do.
- The **seed** (investment): grows on its own with time and care.

Smart financial lives often include a mix of all three, earning through work, building through business, and growing through investing.

Taxes

Whenever money is earned, a portion usually goes to **taxes**. Taxes are a mandatory cost charged by the government, and refusal to pay them will result in significant fines and even imprisonment.

Whether your worldview finds taxes to be a net negative (forced upon you, much of it spent on programs you disagree with) or a net positive (taxes help fund schools, roads, parks, firefighters, and other community services), your responsibility to pay them remains the same. Understanding taxes early helps avoid surprises later.

- **Employees** have taxes taken directly out of their paychecks.
- **Business owners** often pay taxes themselves, usually quarterly, after subtracting expenses.
- **Investors** pay taxes on profits, called *capital gains*.

Learning about taxes isn't just about paying, it's about **planning**. Knowing what portion of income belongs to the government helps you make realistic goals for what's truly yours to spend, save, and give.

Reflection Questions:

- Think about any tax funded services that you use? Which do you appreciate the most?
- Think about any tax funded services that you disagree with. How do you feel about being forced to contribute to it?

Real-World Examples

Adult-Level Examples:

- **Employee:** A teacher earns a salary for the hours spent preparing lessons and teaching.
- **Business Owner:** A local bakery sells 100 loaves of bread a day, earning money while multiple employees work.
- **Investor:** Someone buys stock in that bakery's supply company, earning dividends when the business does well.

Kid & Teen Examples:

- **Employee:** Babysitting for $15 an hour.
- **Business Owner:** Selling custom bracelets online.
- **Investor:** Buying one share of a company that makes art supplies.

Seeing real models helps connect everyday life to these three paths. Every time someone earns, they're using one (or more) of them.

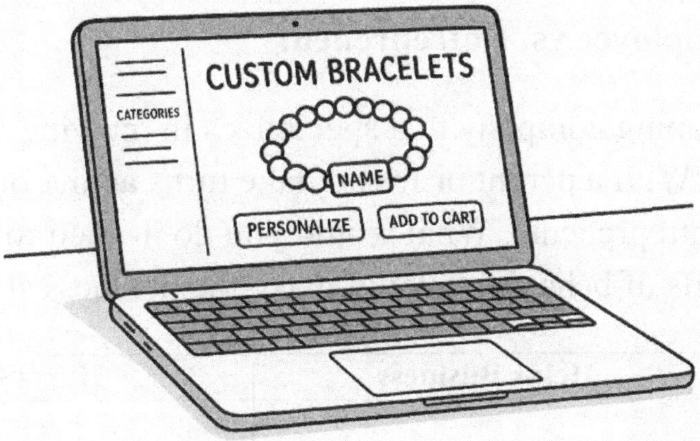

Chapter 3 Reflection Questions:

- Which of the three ways of earning (employee, business owner, investor) feels most interesting to you?
- How might each of these fit into your life now or in the future?
- Which do you think grows fastest, and which feels safest?
- What kind of value do you enjoy creating for others?

Activities: How People Make Money

1. Your First $100 Challenge

Brainstorm how you would earn your first $100 (excluding allowance). Could it come from chores, a small business idea, or something else? Write down your plan, materials needed, and how long you think it would take.

2. Role-Play: Employee vs. Entrepreneur

Imagine a landscaping company that specializes in mowing lawns and planting flowers. With a parent or friend, take turns acting out both roles (employee and entrepreneur). What would you do in each role to make more money? What sorts of behaviors would make the business struggle?

Role	Helps Business	Hurts Business
Employee		
Entrepreneur		

3. The Scaling Ladder: Daymond John

A well-known example of someone who went from working as an employee in his youth to owning his business, then becoming a famous investor is Daymond John. Search for a biographical article about him online, then answer the following questions.

How did Daymond earn money as an employee in his early years?

____

____

____

____

What business did Daymond start? How did he grow it?

____

____

____

____

Name three businesses that Daymond has invested in. How does he make money with them?

Business Name	How Daymond Makes Money on This Investment

Chapter 4: Entrepreneurship in Action

Opening Story: The Case of the Sticky Sidewalk

Every spring, the ice cream shop near Ella's house did booming business…until the afternoon heat hit. Customers would walk outside, take two licks, and realize their cones were melting faster than they could eat them. By the time they reached the curb, their hands were sticky, their napkins shredded, and a trail of melted ice cream marked the sidewalk.

Ella noticed it every year. But this time, instead of walking past, she thought, *what if this is a problem I could solve?*

She experimented at home using scraps of cardboard, paper sleeves, and old craft supplies. After a few tries, she came up with a cone holder that caught drips without leaking. She asked the ice cream shop owner if she could leave a small box of her "DripStoppers" on the counter for customers to buy for 25 cents each. He agreed. By the end of the week, she'd sold out.

Ella didn't just earn money, she **created value**. She solved a real problem for real people, in a way that made life a little better. That's the heart of entrepreneurship.

What Is Entrepreneurship?

At its core, entrepreneurship means **turning ideas into action that create value**. Value can mean solving a problem, saving time, improving comfort, or bringing joy. Entrepreneurs look for needs and find creative ways to meet them.

You don't have to start a giant company to be an entrepreneur. You can start right where you are; with one problem, one idea, and one experiment.

Some businesses grow into companies with employees, stores, and investors. Others stay small and personal, like a single lawn-mowing route or art shop. The size doesn't matter as much as the **mindset**: entrepreneurs see challenges as opportunities.

Here's the magic: every time you trade value for money, you're part of a **mini economy**. You identify what people care about, offer something that helps, and get rewarded for it. The better you understand what people need, the more successful you can become.

Reflection Question:

- What's one small problem in your day-to-day life that you'd love to solve for yourself or for others?

Types of Entrepreneurial Paths

There isn't just one kind of entrepreneurship. Let's explore three main categories that kids, teens, and adults alike can start with.

1. Product Businesses

A product business sells something **tangible** (something you can hold or use). It might be homemade, digital, or even custom-made.

Examples:

- Lemonade stands and bake sales
- Jewelry, stickers, or crafts sold online
- Digital art, printable planners, or e-books
- A store that sells individual items for more than the wholesale/bulk order price they paid (ex. book store, toy store, etc.)
- Handmade soap, candles, or T-shirts

Product businesses often start small but can grow fast if you learn about packaging, pricing, and presentation. The key is to make something people genuinely want and design it so they can easily buy it.

- **Kid Example:** A student sells keychains at school using designs that show team spirit or inside jokes.
- **Teen Example:** A digital artist sells custom phone wallpapers on Etsy.
- **Adult Example:** A local baker turns weekend cupcakes into a catering business.

2. Service Businesses

Service businesses don't sell things, they sell **time, skills, or effort**. The business exists to make someone's life easier or save them from doing something themselves.

Examples:

- Lawn mowing, snow shoveling, or pet sitting
- Tutoring, babysitting, or helping with technology
- Car washing or organizing closets
- Editing videos or taking photos

Services usually cost little to start but require reliability, communication, and good customer experience. Great service creates repeat customers.

- **Kid Example:** A 10-year-old offers to walk a neighbors' dog while they work during the summer.
- **Teen Example:** A 15-year-old offers math tutoring for $15/hour.
- **Adult Example:** A landscaper expands to manage full lawn maintenance across neighborhoods.

3. Creative Businesses

Creative entrepreneurship turns imagination into income. These businesses often blend art, entertainment, and storytelling. Creative businesses can also be product or service businesses.

Examples:

- Graphic design, photography, or illustration
- Blogging, podcasting, or streaming
- Writing stories or music
- Making educational or funny videos

Creative entrepreneurs focus on connecting with audiences and building trust. Their value isn't just the product, it's their **voice** and perspective.

- **Kid Example:** A student writes comics and sells them at school events.
- **Teen Example:** A content creator posts how-to videos for DIY crafts and earns through ad revenue.
- **Adult Example:** A wedding photographer turns a hobby into a full-time career.

From Lemonade Stand to Shark Tank

Every big company starts small. The skills that help you sell lemonade on your street corner are the same skills that can one day help you pitch on Shark Tank or launch your own online store.

Let's take that lemonade stand and see how it can grow:

Stage	Focus	Lesson Learned
1. Homemade	Making and selling to neighbors	Practice pricing, presentation, and friendly communication
2. Neighborhood Brand	Expanding to new blocks, maybe hiring a friend	Learn teamwork and consistency
3. Local Event Booth	Selling at a fair or farmer's market	Practice marketing and inventory management
4. Scaled-Up Business	Creating a website, adding flavors, branding cups, selling drink mixes to grocery chains.	Learn customer experience and reinvestment
5. Shark Tank Level	Pitching to investors or scaling to stores	Master storytelling and growth strategy

The idea isn't that every lemonade stand becomes a company. It's that every entrepreneur starts by seeing *potential* where others see "just a hobby."

Reflection Question:

- Think of something small you've done, like a fundraiser, bake sale, or craft. How could you make it reach more people or run more smoothly?

How Entrepreneurs Think: The Value Creation Mindset

Entrepreneurs ask one key question: **"What problem can I solve?"**

That's it. Every successful business begins by noticing something people need or wish were better. Sometimes those problems are obvious (people are hungry, need clean clothes, or want entertainment). Sometimes they're emotional (people want to feel proud, connected, or understood).

Once you start looking for problems instead of products, your ideas multiply.

Examples of problems kids can solve:

- Younger students need organized study help
- Parents want quick dog walkers after work
- Neighbors want their driveways shoveled in winter
- Families want birthday cards or decorations made locally

Problems are everywhere, and solving them is how value is created.

Reflection Question:

- What's a small problem you've noticed at school or in your community that you could help fix?

The Entrepreneurship Process: From Idea to Profit

Entrepreneurship can seem mysterious, but it's just a repeatable process anyone can learn.

1. Idea: Look for problems to solve or ways to make things better. The best ideas come from observing your world and asking "why not?"

2. Test: Before spending lots of money or time, test your idea on a small scale. Ask for feedback. Try it with a few customers. Make adjustments.

3. Improve: Listen to what works and what doesn't. Maybe your cookies need to be softer, or your service needs faster delivery. Improvement is part of every success story.

4. Sell: Set a fair price, find customers, and offer your product or service with confidence. Selling isn't tricking people; it's helping them see the value you've created.

5. Profit: After covering costs, whatever money is left over is profit. That's what allows your business to grow, or what you can save, invest, or give.

Common Myths About Entrepreneurship

1. **"You need a lot of money to start."**
   False. Many businesses start with creativity, not capital. Start small, use what you have, and scale over time.
2. **"You have to be an adult."**
   False. Many kid and teen entrepreneurs start before high school. What matters is responsibility and follow-through.
3. **"You can't fail."**
   False. Every entrepreneur fails sometimes. The goal isn't to avoid failure, it's to learn fast and adjust.
4. **"You have to invent something brand new."**
   False. Most success comes from improving existing ideas. You don't need to reinvent lemonade, just make the best lemonade stand in town.

Reflection Question:

- Which myth have you believed before? What's changed your mind?

Chapter 4 Reflection Questions

1. What types of businesses do you find most exciting? Product, service, or creative?
2. Think about your community. What's a small problem you could help solve?
3. How could you test an idea before going "all in"?
4. What's one thing you've learned from trying something that didn't work?

Activities: Entrepreneurship in Action

1. Problem Spotter

List three small problems you've noticed this week at school, home, or in your neighborhood. Then brainstorm how you might solve each one.

Problems	How to Solve It
Problem 1:	
Problem 2:	
Problem 3:	

2. The $10 Startup

Pretend you have only $10 to start a business. What kind of business could you launch? What materials would you need, and how would you make your first sale?

____

____

____

____

____

____

____

3. Lemonade Upgrade

Imagine that you are starting a local lemonade stand. Write down how you'd make it stand out. Would you change the recipe, the design, the location, or the experience? Describe what would make your stand "the talk of the town."

Chapter 5: Your Value and Your Skills

Opening Story: Two Employees, Two Outcomes

The new frozen-yogurt shop on Main Street hired two teens on the same day; Marcus and Taylor. Both started at $12 an hour, running the register and cleaning tables.

At first, they seemed alike. But by the end of the first month, everyone noticed the difference.

Marcus always showed up five minutes early, asked customers about their favorite toppings, upsold extra toppings, and helped new staff learn the ropes. When business was slow, he restocked cups, wiped counters, and brainstormed ways to bring in more customers. He even suggested putting the most-popular flavors near the front to cut line times.

Taylor, meanwhile, did the bare minimum. If the manager wasn't watching, he scrolled on his phone. He took longer breaks, ignored small messes, and avoided helping others. After several months, Taylor's hours were cut, and Marcus got promoted to assistant manager with a $3 an hour raise.

Marcus hadn't just worked harder; he'd **added value**. He made the shop better, and the shop rewarded him. That's how the real world works: when you solve more problems, learn more skills, and show reliability, your value grows; and so does your earning potential.

Had the frozen yogurt shop not rewarded him, Marcus would still have accomplished enough to make himself a valuable talent that other stores would be willing to pay more than $12 an hour.

How Wages Are Set

When you get hired, the wage isn't random. It's based on three things:

1. **Market Value**: What similar jobs pay in your area.
2. **Skill Level**: How well you can do the job.
3. **Added Value**: What unique contributions you bring that others don't.

For example, if every ice-cream shop in town pays $12 an hour, that's the *market rate*. But a worker who's dependable, friendly, and efficient can rise above that rate through raises or promotions. Businesses reward the people who make their lives easier or their profits higher.

Even adults face the same equation. Someone who learns new software, improves productivity, or mentors teammates can ask for a raise because they've proven they're worth more.

Reflection Questions:

- Think of a time when someone went "above and beyond" for you. How did it make you feel, and how might an employer feel when you do the same?
- Imagine that you own the frozen yogurt shop that employs Marcus and Taylor. If Taylor were to tell you that another store offered to pay

him more, would you try to match their offer? Would you consider firing him regardless if his performance did not approve?

- Imagine that you own the frozen yogurt shop that employs Marcus and Taylor. If Marcus were to tell you that another store offered to pay him more, would you try to match or beat their offer? If yes, explain why.

Learning Valuable Skills

Your most powerful asset isn't money, it's **skills**. Skills are the tools you carry for life. They make you employable, adaptable, and capable of turning ideas into income.

1. Hard Skills

These are measurable, teachable abilities; like typing, coding, baking, or fixing bikes. Hard skills make you *competent* in a specific area.

2. Soft Skills

These are how you interact; communication, reliability, teamwork, attitude. Soft skills make you *pleasant* to work with, and often matter even more.

In many cases, the top leaders at a big company are not the most skilled performers, but their combination of strong hard skills and soft skills makes them better candidates for leadership than colleagues with excellent hard skills but poor soft skills.

For teens, learning valuable skills might look like:

- Improving grades in subjects tied to future jobs (math, writing, design)
- Taking a trade or tech elective (woodshop, robotics, graphic design)
- Learning to budget, communicate, or lead a group project

For adults, it could mean:

- Mastering a new software program
- Taking a certification course
- Networking or attending workshops

Every skill you add widens your options and raises your value.

Reflection Question:

- What's one skill you already have that could be sharpened to make you stand out?

Reliability and Attitude: Your Daily Reputation

Skills open the door, but reliability and attitude keep it open.

Employers and customers notice who can be counted on. Reliability means doing what you say you'll do, on time, every time. It means being honest about mistakes, asking for help when needed, and finishing tasks without being reminded.

Attitude is equally powerful. Two people can have the same skills, but the one who stays positive during challenges becomes a natural leader. A "can-do" mindset makes you the person others want on their team.

Marcus from the yogurt shop wasn't perfect. He occasionally spilled toppings, forgot napkins, and once mixed up orders, but he owned up, fixed it, and smiled through it. That's what earned him trust.

Reliability + attitude = reputation.
Reputation = opportunity.

Building Reputation and Trust

Reputation is like credit; in that it builds slowly but can be lost fast.

Ways to build it:

- **Show up** consistently.
- **Communicate** clearly (saying "I'll finish this by 5 p.m." and do it).
- **Take ownership** by fixing mistakes rather than hiding them.
- **Help others** without being asked.

Each small action signals, "*you can count on me*".

Trust doesn't require fancy achievements; it requires follow-through. When adults write job references or recommend people, they talk about trust more than talent.

Reflection Question:

- If someone described your reputation in one sentence, what would you want them to say?

How to Earn More Over Time

Even in the same job, not everyone earns the same. Here's how to increase your potential wherever you are:

1. **Be Curious.** Learn how the whole system works, not just your part. Understanding big-picture goals lets you spot ways to improve them.
2. **Take Initiative.** See something that needs doing? Do it. Suggest ideas politely.
3. **Learn and Adapt.** Technology and tools change, so stay open to new ones.
4. **Build Relationships.** Coworkers and mentors can open doors you didn't know existed.
5. **Track Your Wins.** Keep notes on tasks you've improved or challenges you've solved. When it's time to ask for a raise, you'll have evidence.

This works at any age. A teen who keeps track of grades and projects can show parents why they've earned more allowance. An adult can show a manager the measurable results of their contributions.

The Economics of Value

In simple terms, you get paid for **the value you create**.

Value = the difference between what you contribute and what others can replace.

If you bring energy, reliability, and problem-solving that others can't (or won't), you become harder to replace, and your wage potential rises.

In many roles, employers expect to make more money by having you than they pay to employ you. If a car dealership hires a salesman, they expect him to earn the dealership more from the sales he makes than his wages cost him. If it were the other way around, it would not make sense for the dealership to keep him employed.

Now, imagine if that dealership hires two salesmen at the same time. After a year, one has sold $3 million worth of cars, while the other has sold $1 million. The salesman who sold $3 million has provided much more value, and will be paid more than his lower performing counterpart.

Employers and customers think in these terms:

“Is this person saving me time, stress, or money?”
“Are they making my business or day run smoother?”

When the answer is yes, value goes up and so does compensation.

That’s why “bare minimum” never wins long term. You might keep your job, but you won’t keep momentum. Value creators always rise.

The Skill Compounding Effect

Skills compound just like money.
When you combine two or more abilities, your value multiplies, not adds.

For example:

- Writing + design = marketing potential
- Math + communication = finance or teaching potential
- Coding + creativity = game design potential

Over years, each new skill acts like *interest* on your career.
That's why lifelong learning isn't optional, it's the key to freedom.

Real-World Examples

Adults:

- A nurse learns a new medical software and earns a promotion.
- A plumber gets certified for eco-friendly installations and charges higher rates.
- A designer learns video editing and adds new clients without more hours.

Teens:

- A student improves grades and earns a scholarship (saving thousands).
- A teen who volunteers at events builds connections that lead to part-time work.
- A high-schooler creates a small app for friends and learns coding skills that land a future internship.

The lesson: every new skill or act of initiative is a seed that grows future income.

Negotiation and Confidence

When you've proven your value, it's okay to **ask** for more.
Negotiation isn't being greedy, it's communicating worth respectfully.

Tips for a Good Conversation

- Be prepared. Know what similar roles pay.
- Be specific. Mention how you've helped or improved results.
- Be positive. "I've really enjoyed this role and would love to grow in it. Could we discuss an increase based on my contributions?"
- Be helpful. "How can I provide more value for this company to warrant an increase in pay and responsibilities?"
- Be patient. Even if the answer is "not yet," you've planted the idea.

For kids and teens, this same approach applies when asking for more allowance or pay for extra chores. Show evidence of effort, responsibility, and results.

Chapter 5 Reflection Questions

1. What's one skill you could learn this year to earn more later?
2. How does attitude influence opportunity?
3. Why do some employees earn more than others in the same job?
4. Which habits would make you the Marcus of your workplace (or household)?

Activities: Your Value and Your Skills

1. Skill Goal Worksheet

Choose one skill (ex. communication, design, writing, advertising) you want to start developing this month. How do you plan to learn/develop it? Write down a time when you will begin doing so.

Skill	How to Learn It	When You'll Start

2. Raise or Allowance Practice

Role-play asking for a raise (or higher allowance). Include what you've done to deserve it, specific examples of reliability and growth, and a clear, respectful ask.

Parents can respond with questions or conditions to practice real conversation skills.

Describe how this conversation went. Were you able to convince them to increase your pay? If yes, how? If not, what could you do to convince them to in a few months from now?

3. Marcus vs. Taylor Analysis

List three differences between Marcus and Taylor. Then write how those habits show up in your own life. Where can you improve your "Marcus moments"?

Difference #1:

____

____

Difference #2:

____

____

Difference #3:

____

____

How these habits show up in my life:

____

____

____

____

____

____

Part 3: Managing Money

Chapter 6: Budgeting Basics

Opening Story: Where Did All the Money Go?

When Jacob got his first real paycheck from his part-time job, he couldn't believe the number on it; $400! For the first time, he felt rich.

Two weeks later, his wallet was empty. Between drive-thru lunches, gas, a new hoodie, new shoes, and a game subscription, the money vanished. "I don't even know where it went," he said.

His older sister, Maya, showed him her spreadsheet. "Every dollar I earn already has a job," she explained.

"Rent, groceries, savings, even a little for fun. If I don't tell my dollars what to do, they run away."

That's the first rule of budgeting: **every dollar should have a job.**

The Core Principle: Every Dollar Has a Job

Budgeting isn't about restriction, it's about direction. If you earn $100, that's 100 chances to make intentional choices.

- Some dollars pay for needs (food, shelter, transportation).
- Some dollars serve goals (savings, giving, investments).
- Some dollars fund wants (entertainment, hobbies, treats).

When each dollar is assigned before you spend it, surprise shortages disappear. Budgeting turns "Where did it go?" into "I know exactly where it went, and why."

Even kids can use this idea. If you get $20 allowance, you might split it like:

- $10 for savings (goal fund)
- $5 for spending (fun money)
- $3 for giving
- $2 for future surprises

It's not the amount that matters most, it's the habit.

Different Budgeting Systems

There's no single "right" method. What matters is choosing one that fits your lifestyle.

1. Zero-Sum Budget

Every dollar is assigned a purpose, where income minus expenses equals zero.

If you earn $2,000 and plan $1,900 in expenses, the remaining $100 must go somewhere (savings, debt repayment, etc.).

Nothing is "extra." This system creates total clarity but takes daily tracking.

2. 50/20/20/10 Rule

A simpler formula for how to assign a role for every dollar you earn:

- 50% Needs (rent, utilities, food)
- 20% Wants (going out, subscriptions)
- 20% Savings or debt repayment
- 10% Giving or charity

It works well for busy families and teens learning to budget for the first time.

3. Envelope Method

An old-school favorite that still works. You divide cash into labeled envelopes like "Groceries," "Gas," and "Fun." When an envelope's empty, you stop spending in that category until next payday. Today, digital "envelopes" apps do the same thing.

Visual Example: The Adult Budget

Let's look at a sample monthly budget for a recent college graduate earning $4,000 take-home pay. Here we will compare a typical budget from an adult who does not closely monitor their expenses against a smart budget used by someone who pays close attention to their expenses and changes their behaviors to save money.

Category	Typical Budget	Smart Budget	Notes
Housing (Rent or Mortgage)	$1,800	$1,400	Moved to a smaller apartment or got a roommate
Transportation	$600	$450	Carpool or public transit saves gas
Food & Dining	$700	$550	Meal planning reduces waste
Utilities	$250	$250	Unchanged
Subscriptions & Entertainment	$200	$100	Cut unused apps
Savings & Investments	$150	$500	Automated savings plan
Giving / Charity	$100	$100	Purposeful generosity
Miscellaneous	$200	$150	Kept small flex fund
Totals	**$4,000**	**$4,000**	Every dollar has a job

The "smart" budget doesn't feel deprived, it just reflects **priorities.** It directs money toward future freedom instead of friction.

Housing Costs — Rent vs. Buy

Housing is usually the biggest expense in any budget. Understanding the trade-offs between renting and owning is critical for future decisions.

Renting

- **Pros:** Flexible, low upfront costs, no maintenance responsibility.
- **Cons:** Does not build equity (you don't own it); rent can rise each year.

Renting is like borrowing space for a while; it's great for mobility or short-term situations. You pay for convenience and freedom.

Buying

- **Pros:** Builds equity as you pay off the loan; stability; potential long-term appreciation.
- **Cons:** High upfront costs (down payment, closing fees); hidden ongoing expenses (interest, property taxes, insurance, HOA fees, repairs).

Buying is like planting roots; you own a piece of your future, but you must maintain it.

Real World Example

Imagine a newlywed couple living in the suburbs of a big city (Chicago in this case). They are trying to decide whether to rent an apartment or buy their first home together.

They want a place with at least three bedrooms to give them space for the family they would like to build, and somewhere within an hour of the city where they work.

In their search, they found a house they like in Waukegan, IL for $205,000, and an apartment they like in Gurnee, IL for $2,000. They decide to compare costs assuming that their potential mortgage would be a 15-year fixed rate mortgage at 5.63%.

Below is the comparison chart they put together weighing three options; renting, buying the home with no money down, or buying the home after using their savings on a down payment that covers 20% the price of the home ($41,000). This number is significant because they are no longer required to pay for private mortgage insurance (PMI) once they have paid off 20% of the home.

In addition to calculating their monthly cost, they want to know how much of their monthly payment is going towards equity in their home vs. how much is going towards costs that do not convert to equity (mortgage interest, taxes, insurance, repairs, and more).

Expense	Rent	Own ($0 down)	Own (20% Down)
Monthly Payment	$2,000	$1,688 (includes $727 principal)	$1,350 (includes $606 principal)
Property Taxes	-	$331	$331
Insurance	Renter $25	$75+$128 PMI	$75
Maintenance/ Repairs	-	$200 avg	$200 avg
HOA Fees	-	$100	$100
Total Monthly Cost	**$2,025**	**$2,522**	**$2,056**
Monthly Cost (no equity)	**$2,025**	**$1,795 (year 1)**	**$1,450 (year 1)**

Note: Monthly cost (no equity) could go down over time as the mortgage payment balances more towards principal (equity) than interest as more payments are made.

As you can see, there is not a clear and obvious winner here. If they choose to rent, they will have the lowest monthly cost, but also spend the most money that does not convert to equity in the long term.

If they do not have a large amount of money saved for a down payment, they would have the largest monthly cost, but would spend less on non-equity housing expenses than they would if they rented, unless they need a major repair (flooded basement, new HVAC system, etc.).

If they were able to save enough for the down payment, they would be doing much better than the average young couple, and buying the home with a down payment would be an attractive option.

If they only have $5,000 in savings between them, they may decide to rent for a few years while saving up for a down payment in the future, and buy a home when they are comfortable with their savings in the future.

There's no universal winner, just different priorities.

- Renting = flexibility.
- Buying = long-term investment and responsibility.

Reflection Questions:

- What matters most to you? Flexibility, ownership, or long-term growth?
- If you were in the Chicago couple's position, what would you choose if you only had $5,000 in savings? What if you had $50,000 in savings?

Tips for Kids and Teens

You can practice budgeting long before you have bills.

- Ask your parents about monthly household costs. (You'll be surprised how many different bills there are!)
- Make a mini-budget for your own money.
- If you earn $20 a week, pretend you "owe" yourself a few mini-bills: $10 for savings, $5 for fun, $3 for giving, and $2 for emergency.
- Plan for surprises, because life always has them.

Budgeting is less about math and more about **awareness**.
Once you know where your money goes, you gain power over it.

Reflection Question:

- Where could you redirect $10 this month to something that matters more? Are there any areas where you feel that your budget is being wasteful? Are there areas where you would like to put more money?

Chapter 6 Reflection Questions

1. Why is it important for every dollar to have a job?
2. Which budgeting system do you think would work best for you and why?
3. What's the biggest advantage of renting? What's the biggest advantage of owning?
4. How does understanding budgets make you feel more in control of your money?

Activities: Budgeting Basics

1. Budget Worksheet

Create a simple budget for a month. If you don't have income yet, pretend you earn $100. Decide how much you'll spend, save, and give. Make sure your total equals exactly $100, because every dollar needs a job.

Use	Spend	Save	Give
Where it Goes			
$ Amount	$	$	$

2. Cash Envelope Simulation

Label three envelopes: *Needs*, *Wants*, *Savings*. Whenever you get money, divide it among them. When a category runs out, that type of spending pauses until next "payday." Try this for one month and see how your spending changes.

Describe how this worked for you. Did you find it to be helpful? Were you able to keep your spending under control?

____

____

____

____

____

____

____

3. Smart Spender Challenge

Look at your last five purchases (allowance or real spending). Which ones were "needs" and which were "wants"?

Pick one want to skip next time and reallocate that money to savings or giving.

Item Purchased	Need or Want?

Chapter 7: Smart Spending

Opening Story: The Mystery of the Empty Account

Every Friday, Chloe looked forward to her after-school smoothie. It was just five bucks; nothing major. But one day, while checking her debit-card app, she froze. Her balance had dropped from $150 to $23. She scrolled through the list: smoothies, coffee runs, late-night delivery, app subscriptions, one new hoodie, and a movie rental.

None of those purchases were "bad" on their own, but together they were a leak in her financial boat.

She told her older brother, who smiled. "You don't have a spending problem," he said. "You have a *budgeting* problem. Smart spending isn't about saying no to everything, it's about *saying yes on purpose*."

Wants vs. Needs

A **need** keeps you functioning. A **want** keeps life fun. Both belong in your budget, but in different proportions.

Needs = food, housing, clothing, transportation, education.
Wants = snacks, games, decorations, gadgets, and upgrades.

Mistaking wants as needs is a common mistake that can lead to people straying from their budget. While food is a **need**, you may **want** a nice lunch from the local sandwich shop instead of preparing a healthy and more affordable meal at home.

Smart spenders pause before buying and ask:

1. Do I need it or just want it?
2. Can I fill this need in a more cost-effective way?
3. Can I afford it without borrowing?
4. Will I still be glad I bought this next week?

A quick 10-second pause can save hundreds over time. The goal isn't to eliminate wants, it's to choose them intentionally.

Marketing and Emotional Spending

Every advertisement you see is designed to make you feel something; urgency, excitement, belonging.

Marketers know how to trigger emotion so you associate spending with happiness. "Limited Time Only!" "Everyone has this now!" "You deserve it!"

Smart spenders step back and recognize those emotional pulls. Before clicking *Buy Now*, ask:

- Am I buying this to solve a problem or to feel better?
- Am I reacting to boredom or pressure?
- Would I still buy it if nobody saw it?

Emotion fades fast; the bill stays.

Reflection Question:

- Think of one time you bought something impulsively. How did you feel the next day?

The Hidden Costs of Subscriptions

Subscriptions are sneaky. They don't *ask* for money each time; they quietly take it every month. Streaming, music, apps, gyms, boxes, and memberships can drain hundreds of dollars a year.

Example:

Five $10 subscriptions = $50 per month = $600 per year.

That's enough for a new phone, a short trip, or part of a savings fund.

Do a quick "subscription audit" every few months. If you haven't used one lately, cancel it and redirect the money somewhere that matters more.

Credit Cards vs. Debit Cards

Debit Cards

Debit cards pull money directly from your account. When you spend, the money leaves immediately. Most debit cards have similar fraud protections to credit cards.

Pros:

- No debt or interest.
- Great for budgeting; you can't spend what isn't there.

Cons:

- Doesn't build credit history.
- Usually has no rewards program.

Credit Cards

Credit cards *loan* you money temporarily. If you pay in full each month, they can be convenient and rewarding. If you don't, they become expensive fast.

Typical yearly/annual interest rates (APR) will be between 15 – 30%. That means unpaid balances grow quickly every month.

Pros:

- Builds credit history
- Often have rewards programs that offer cash back or vouchers for travel expenses.
- Allow you to pay for emergencies that you do not have immediate cash to cover.

Cons:

- Puts user in debt at a high interest rate
- Easy to overspend your budget since purchases don't directly pull money from your account.
- Credit card companies design their programs to encourage people to spend more and take on interest.

The $1,000 Purchase That Costs $1,400

If you charge $1,000 and only make minimum payments at 20% interest, you'll spend roughly $400 extra in interest and take over three years to finish paying.

That's like paying *$40 a month for 36 months*, for something that might not even last that long.

Choosing Wisely

Credit cards can help build credit history and provide you with rewards bonuses if you're disciplined. However, for most beginners, debit cards offer peace of mind and simplicity.

Debt averse financial experts including Dave Ramsey recommend against credit card use. Their case will cite human psychology, noting that most people think they will use them correctly, but statistics show that most do not and end up in debt.

They will also note that building credit is only useful if you intend to take out future loans. If you were to apply for an automotive loan to buy a new car, a strong credit score will help you secure the loan, and at a more friendly rate. If you saved up to buy the car with cash, your credit score would be irrelevant in the transaction.

Even if you largely agree with these arguments, you may find that it is beneficial to have a credit card that you only use on purchases you were already going to make, and pay the balance in full before interest can accrue.

An adult may choose to use a debit card for most purchases that tempt impulse buys (ex. department store, groceries, etc.) but use a credit card on regular purchases they would have to make regardless (gym dues, energy bill, gas, etc.).

Credit cards do have unique benefits over debit cards, but you must have a plan and stay disciplined to ensure that using them is a net positive.

Reflection Question:

- Would you rather only use a debit card, only use a credit card, or use both for different purchases? Why?

Unit Pricing and Comparison Shopping

Have you ever seen two boxes of cereal, one twice the size but only $1 more? Which is the better deal?

That's where **unit pricing** comes in. It shows cost per ounce, pound, or item.

If a 16-ounce box is $4 and an 8-ounce box is $3:

- $4 ÷ 16 = 25¢ per ounce.
- $3 ÷ 8 = 37.5¢ per ounce.

The bigger box is the better value. If you were planning to use 16 ounces, you would save $2 by buying the big box. However, if you were only going to use 8 ounces, it would make more sense to buy the small box for $3 than buying the big one and throwing out the extra food.

Comparison shopping is like budget exercise; it builds money muscles. You learn to spend based on value, not marketing.

Quality vs. Quantity

Buying cheap isn't always saving. Sometimes a $20 item that lasts five years beats a $10 item that breaks in six months. Smart spending means balancing price and durability.

Ask:

- Will this last?
- Will I use it often enough to justify the cost?
- Is this something I could borrow or buy used?

Learning when to buy quality items on purpose is a superpower that saves thousands over a lifetime.

Visual: The True Cost of a Latte Habit

Many college students and working adults make a habit of going to their favorite coffee shop and getting a coffee or tea each morning before work or school. For just $5 each day, they get a satisfying boost of energy to jump start the day.

Although $5 does not sound like much, it can add up very quickly. One $5 coffee per weekday = $25 per week ≈ $100 per month ≈ $1,200 per year.

Imagine if a coffee loving adult decided to start brewing coffee at home instead of going to the coffee shop each morning. Instead of each cup costing $5, the home brewed coffee only costs $0.50 per weekday. One $0.50 coffee per weekday = $2.50 per week ≈ $10 per month ≈ $120 per year.

In your budget, $1 saved is as good as $1 earned. In saving $1,080 per year, this man effectively gave himself a $0.54 per hour raise if he works 40 hours per week.

And it gets better. Imagine if he invested the $90 per month that he saved by brewing his coffee at home. At a 7% return for 10 years, he would have about **$15,400**.

That's not to say you can never go to your local coffee shop, it's a reminder that small habits become big results over time.

Reflection Question:

- What's one small purchase you could pause this week, and what goal could that money support instead?

Tips for Kids and Teens

- Track your spending for a week. Notice where money "leaks."
- Ask your parents how they decide between brands or services.
- Practice saying "I'll think about it" before buying. Most impulse wants fade within a day.
- Remember: you can say yes to almost anything, just not everything at once.

Chapter 7 Reflection Questions:

1. How do advertisers influence your spending choices?
2. What's one subscription or habit you could cut to save money?
3. Would you prefer a credit card with rewards or a debit card with safety? Why?
4. How do you decide between quality and price when buying something?

Activities: Smart Spending

1. Smart Shopper Scavenger Hunt

Visit a store (or browse online) and compare three items that serve the same purpose. Record price, size, and cost per unit. Which is the best value, and why?

Examples: 43” 4K TVs, toasters, or canned chicken noodle soup.

Items	Price	Size	Cost per Unit
	$		$
	$		$
	$		$

2. Family Spending Challenge

With your family, find three ways to save money this month.

Examples: cancel unused subscriptions, pack lunch twice a week, or shop with a list.

Add up the monthly savings and decide where to redirect them (savings, charity, family fun).

____

____

____

____

____

____

3. Interest-Cost Calculator

Pretend you charged $500 on a credit card at 20% interest and paid only $25 a month. Tip: You can use an online amortization calculator looking at a $500 balance at 20% interest over 2 years, with $25 monthly payments.

How much extra would you pay in interest? ______________________________

Discuss how that money could be used instead.

____

____

____

____

____

____

Chapter 8: Saving and Emergency Funds

Opening Story: The Flat Tire Fund

When Richard finally bought his first used car, it felt like freedom. Windows down, music up, independence at last. But then…*thump*. A flat tire on a rainy night.

The replacement cost? $140. Richard checked his account and only saw $47. He ended up borrowing money from his parents, promising to pay them back after his next few paychecks.

That's when his dad smiled and said, "This is why we have what I call the *Flat Tire Fund.* Life happens. Savings turn emergencies into inconveniences instead of crises."

From that night on, Richard started setting aside a few dollars from each paycheck. Months later, when his phone battery died, he didn't stress; he just used his *emergency fund.*

Saving, he realized, wasn't about deprivation. It was about **peace of mind.**

Why Saving Matters

Saving isn't about hoarding money, it's about **freedom**. When you save, you give yourself options. You can handle the unexpected, say yes to opportunities, and avoid panic when surprises hit.

Think of savings as your personal safety net. Without one, a small problem can turn into a big setback. With one, you stay steady and confident.

Saving also brings emotional peace. Instead of worrying about "what if," you know you're ready for "when." Whether it's car repairs, doctor bills, broken phones, or last-minute school fees, these things will happen. Savings make them manageable.

Reflection Question:

- What is the most memorable surprise expense that you had to pay for or needed help with?

Three Kinds of Savings

Every smart saver builds three "money buckets." Each one has a different purpose and time horizon.

1. Short-Term Savings

These are goals you plan to reach within a few months or a year; like a new gadget, trip, or special event. Short-term savings teach discipline and delayed gratification.

Examples:

- A $200 tablet

- A $150 trip with friends
- $50 for holiday gifts

Short-term savings help you practice success in small steps.

2. Long-Term Savings

These are the "big future goals"; college, a car, a down payment on a future home, or retirement. They often require more patience, consistency, and compounding interest.

Adults usually set up automatic transfers to long-term retirement accounts like 401(k)s or IRAs. Teens can start early by saving a percentage of any income, including birthday money, side jobs, or part-time work.

Example:

Saving $25 a week from age 15 could turn into **tens of thousands** by adulthood through interest and investing.

3. Emergency Savings

Your emergency fund is the financial equivalent of a superhero shield. It steps in when life throws surprises.

The goal: 3–6 months of expenses once you're earning regularly.
For kids and teens, even a few hundred dollars can be enough for small "emergencies" like phone repairs or helping with school costs.

Start small. Even $10 a week adds up to over $500 a year, plus the calm of knowing you're covered.

Reflection Question:

- Which of these savings types do you think you could start today? How much could you begin with?

Where to Keep Your Savings

Choosing the right place for your money is part of saving wisely. There's no one perfect spot; it depends on your goals.

Type	Best For	How It Works	Average Return (2025)
Regular Checking Account	Spending money	Easy access, but earns little or no interest	~0.1%
High-Yield Savings Account (HYSA)	Emergency or short-term goals	FDIC-insured, safe, pays much higher interest than checking	4–5%
Money Market Account	Flexible savings	Slightly higher interest; limited transactions	3–4%
Certificate of Deposit (CD)	Long-term, no-touch goals	Locks money for a set time (6–24 months); higher interest	4–5.5%

HYSAs are especially good for emergency funds; you earn interest, but still have access when you need it. CDs usually work best for money you *won't touch* for a while.

Interest rates change over time, and move in tandem with the Federal Reserve rate. When the Fed increases rates, interest rates on loans increase, but so do interest rates on savings accounts.

Visual: The Power of Consistent Saving

Imagine you save just $50 a month starting at age 15 and earn 5% annual compounding interest.

Years Saved	Total You Deposited	Total with Interest
1	$600	$615
5	$3,000	$3,400
10	$6,000	$7,700
20	$12,000	**$19,800**

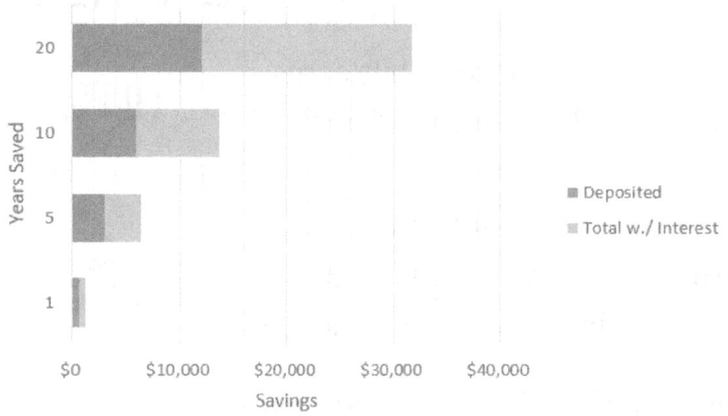

Saving small amounts consistently beats saving big amounts occasionally. Time is your financial superpower.

How to Start Saving (Even When It Feels Impossible)

1. **Pay Yourself First:** Treat saving like a bill you owe *your future self.* Move the money right after you get paid.
2. **Automate It:** Set up auto-transfers to a savings account so you don't have to rely on willpower.
3. **Make It Visual:** Track your progress on paper or a spreadsheet. Watching the balance grow feels rewarding.

4. **Name Your Accounts:** "Trip Fund," "Emergency Fund," "Car Fund." When your money has a purpose, it's easier to protect.
5. **Save Windfalls:** Got birthday money, a tax refund, or an unexpected gift? Save at least part of it before spending.
6. **Celebrate Milestones:** Every $50, $100, or $500 saved deserves a small celebration. The habit matters more than the amount.

The Psychology of Saving

Saving triggers something powerful in your brain, shifting you from **reactive** to **proactive.** Instead of waiting for life to happen to you, you're preparing for it. That builds confidence.

Saving also teaches delayed gratification, one of the best predictors of long-term success. Saving gives you the ability to wait now for something better later.

Finally, saving helps reduce stress. Knowing you're prepared allows you to focus on what really matters instead of worrying about "what if."

Reflection Question:

- What would you feel proud to buy, fix, or fund someday with your savings?

Tips for Kids and Teens

- Label jars or envelopes for different goals (Spend, Save, Give, Grow).
- Use a savings app or notebook to track progress.
- Save part of any money you receive; 10% is a great start.
- Watch your savings "grow bar" each month and set mini goals.

Even if your income is small, your consistency isn't. Every dollar saved proves you're in control.

Real-World Example: The Emergency Buffer

Meet Alicia, 23, living in the Chicago suburbs with $3,200 take-home pay. She built an emergency fund of $3,000 by saving $250 a month for a year.

When her car's transmission failed, the repair cost $1,200. Instead of panic, credit card debt, or borrowing, she paid cash and still had $1,800 left.

She said afterward, "My emergency fund turned a nightmare into an inconvenience."

That's exactly what saving is for; not perfection, but protection.

Chapter 8 Reflection Questions

1. What are three reasons saving money helps reduce stress?
2. Which type of savings (short-term, long-term, or emergency) do you want to focus on first?
3. What does "pay yourself first" mean to you?
4. How could you automate your savings starting this month?

Activities: Saving and Emergency Funds

1. Save the Change Challenge

Grab a jar and label it "Change for My Future." Every time you get coins or small bills, drop them in. When it's full, count it and decide whether to start or boost an emergency fund.

How much money was in the jar? ______________________________

What will you do with this money?

____

____

____

2. Short-Term Goal Simulation

Pick any $100 item (or group of items) you want. If you save $10 per week, how long would it take to afford it?

Item(s):

____

How long would it take to afford it? ____________________________

How does that feel compared to buying it instantly on credit?

____

____

____

____

Part 4: Debt

Chapter 9: Understanding Debt

Opening Story: The Price of "Later"

Ethan had been eyeing a gaming laptop for months. It cost $1,200, which was way more than he had saved. At the store, a bright sign offered *"Buy Now, Pay Later (BNPL) For Only $50 a Month!"* It sounded perfect. He signed up for the store credit plan, brought the laptop home, and bragged to his friends about his deal.

Three months later, the first "interest" charge hit because he hadn't fully paid it off in time. By the end of the year, that $1,200 laptop had cost over $1,500. The store had gotten paid, the BNPL company got $300 in interest, and Ethan had learned a lesson.

What Is Debt?

Debt means borrowing money today and promising to repay it later, usually with interest. Interest on debt is the price you pay to borrow money now.

Debt can help people achieve goals they couldn't afford all at once (like a car, college, or a house). It can also trap people when used carelessly.

The Golden Rule:

Debt should move you forward, not hold you back.

When used wisely, debt can be a tool. When misused, it becomes a burden that steals from your future.

Examples:

A **wise** usage of debt would be an affordable mortgage on a starter home that you put a 20%+ down payment on.

An **unwise** usage of debt would be Ethan's laptop purchased on a high interest buy now, pay later program.

Good Debt vs. Bad Debt

Not all debt is equal. Some debts can increase your opportunities, while others quietly drain your resources.

Type of Debt	Example	Why People Use It	Potential Risk
Good Debt	Some business loans, some mortgages	Builds assets or income over time	Overspending or poor planning can turn good debt bad
Bad Debt	Credit card debt, payday loans, car loans on luxury models	Spends money on things that lose value	High interest traps borrowers for years

Good debt helps you grow your future, and has well-defined plan to pay it off. A small business that needs some money this month to cover the cost of filling a big order that they will be paid for next month is taking on good debt (as long as terms are fair).

Bad debt pays for today at tomorrow's expense, and often does not have a well-defined plan for when and how it will be paid off. By the time that it is paid off, the person who takes on bad debt will likely feel regret.

Reflection Question:

- What's one thing you'd never want to borrow for?

How Interest Works

Interest is the fee you pay for using someone else's money.
If you borrow $100 at 10% annual interest, you owe $110 after a year.

Simple interest = Principal × Rate × Time.

But most debts use **compound interest**, meaning interest is charged on the interest too. Over time, that makes debt grow like a snowball rolling downhill.

Example:

If you borrow $10,000 at 20% interest and pay only the minimum each month, you could end up paying nearly **$4,000 in extra interest** before it's gone. Rather than the final amount paid being 20% of $10,000 ($2,000; simple interest), you would be paying twice as much due to the interest compounding.

Minimum Payments and the Trap of Time

Credit card companies often require only a **minimum payment** (often 2–3% of your balance). It sounds helpful, but it stretches out repayment dramatically. In doing so, the credit card companies can make much more interest on your remaining balance if you choose to pay the minimum.

Amortization Example

Suppose you owe $10,000 at 18% interest.

Payment Per Month	Time to Pay Off	Total Interest Paid
$200	6 years	$4,200
$400	2.8 years	$1,500
$800	1.2 years	$780

Paying more than the minimum saves years of remaining in debt and thousands of dollars. Debt doesn't just cost money; it costs *time.*

Strategies To Pay Off Debt

When paying off multiple debts, two popular strategies stand out:

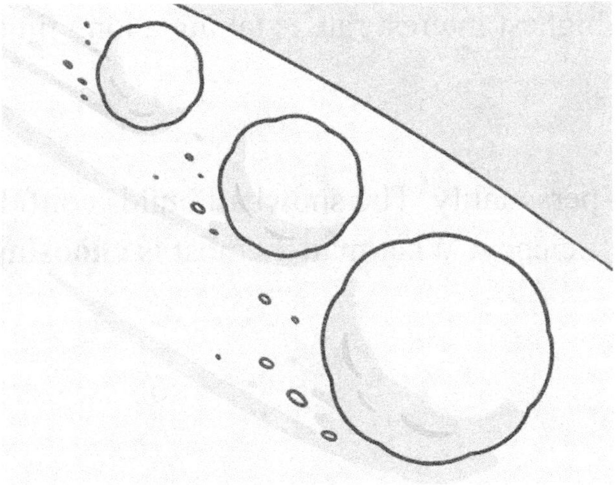

Debt Snowball (Dave Ramsey Method)

1. List debts from smallest balance to largest.
2. Pay minimums on all but the smallest.
3. Attack the smallest debt aggressively until it's gone.
4. Roll that payment into the next smallest one; your "snowball" grows.

Why it works:

Although much of personal finance comes down to logic and numbers, emotions and psychology also play a major role. This strategy lets you see quick wins and stay motivated.

Credit Avalanche

1. List debts from highest interest rate to lowest.
2. Pay off the one with the highest rate first.
3. Save more money long-term because less interest accumulates.

Why it works:

You minimize total cost and pay less over time. This strategy is more mathematically correct than the Debt Snowball, but can be discouraging if your debt with the highest interest rate is taking a long time to pay in full.

Which is better?

It depends on your personality. The snowball builds confidence; the avalanche builds efficiency. What matters most is **choosing a method and sticking with it.**

The Emotional Side of Debt

Debt affects more than bank accounts; it shapes emotions and behavior. People in debt often feel trapped or guilty, even if they're managing fine. But paying off debt brings relief, confidence, and a sense of freedom.

When you're in debt, it can feel like the money that you earn is working against you, as interest compounds in the lender's favor. When you're debt free, you can save or invest the money you once spent on debt payments, making interest compound in your favor.

Reflection Question:

- How would you feel if you were completely debt-free?

Taxes and Debt

Taxes and debt often intertwine.

- Mortgage interest and some student loan interest can reduce taxable income for adults.
- Credit card and personal loan interest are *not* tax-deductible.

A common misconception is that it's better to hold on to debt that reduces taxable income. Imagine that Ethan decided to pay the minimum balance on his student loans to get a larger income tax break. By the end of the year, he pays $5,000 in interest, saving him $1,500 in income taxes.

It can be easy to look at the $1,500 saved as a big win, but he will end up having to pay $3,500 from the prior year between interest and taxes, and have a higher remaining balance.

If Ethan decided to pay extra on his student loans, he may end up having to pay $3,000 in interest at the end of the year, saving him $900 in income taxes. Between interests and income taxes, he will end up having to pay $2,100 from the prior year between interest and taxes.

If you only compare the $1,500 tax savings to the $900 savings, it would look like Ethan made a $600 mistake by aggressively paying off his student loans. When you look at the total between interest and taxes, you see that Ethan made a great choice by paying extra, saving $1,400.

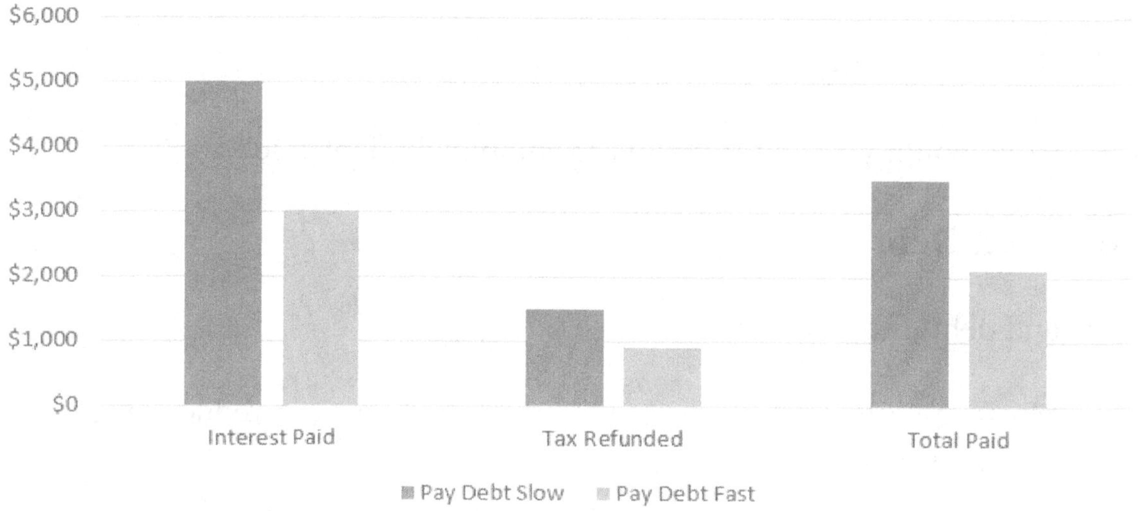

As it turns out, hanging on to tax deductible interest is like trading dollars (interest) for dimes (tax savings).

It's another reminder: understanding how debt interacts with taxes helps people make smarter decisions.

Avoiding the Debt Spiral

1. **Borrow only what you can repay.**
   Just because a lender offers $10,000 doesn't mean you need it.

2. **Know your interest rate.**
   Always read the fine print; 15% vs. 25% interest changes everything.
3. **Pay more than the minimum.**
   Paying extra each month cuts time and cost drastically.
4. **Think before financing.**
   Ask: "Will this item still be valuable when I finish paying for it?"
5. **Avoid lifestyle debt.**
   Debt for clothes, vacations, or eating out is rarely worth it.

Visual: Interest Rates on a $10,000 Loan

Let's look at how interest adds up when you pay $200 per month:

Interest Rate	Years to Pay Off	Total Cash Paid
5%	4.6	$11,000
10%	5.7	$13,700
18%	7.8	$18,800
25%	10.2	$24,400

That means you would pay **$14,400** more at 25% than at 5% on the same $10,000 borrowed!

Interest is the silent partner in every loan. The higher it is, the more it eats away your future income.

Chapter 9 Reflection Questions:

1. What's the difference between good debt and bad debt?
2. How can paying more than the minimum save you time and money?
3. Why do you think people sometimes take on debt they can't afford?

Activities: Understanding Debt

1. Amortization Challenge

Pretend you borrow $10,000 at 15% interest. Use an online calculator to see what happens if you pay $500/month vs. $200/month. Record how long it takes to pay off and how much interest you save by paying more monthly.

Monthly Payment	Time to Pay Off	Interest Paid
$500 per month		**$**
$200 per month		**$**
Difference		**$**

2. Snowball vs. Avalanche Simulation

Imagine having the three debts below:

Debt	Balance	Interest Rate	Minimum Payment
Credit Card	$1,000	20%	$25
Car Loan	$5,000	7%	$200
Student Loan	$10,000	9%	$300

Try both methods (snowball and avalanche), assuming that you have an extra $250 in your budget each month after covering minimum payments ($525):

Compare total time and cost. Which feels more motivating to you?

____

____

____

____

3. Family Debt Discussion

Ask an adult how they decide whether something is worth borrowing for. Record their best advice and one lesson they learned about debt.

Chapter 10: Two Ways to Handle Debt

Opening Story: Two Friends, Two Paths

When Maya and Leo graduated from college, they both had about $25,000 in student loans.

Maya decided to live simply, pay off her debt as fast as possible, and avoid borrowing again.

Leo took a different route. He kept his student loan payments small while saving to buy a duplex. He lived in one half and rented out the other.

Ten years later, Maya was completely debt-free and loved the peace that came with it. As each month passed, her savings and investments continued to grow.

Leo still had some debt, but he also owned three small properties. His rental income covered his mortgage, and helped him work towards acquiring another property.

Two friends, two philosophies. Neither one was necessarily "wrong."

This chapter will explore both mindsets, and help you decide which one fits you best.

Two Famous Approaches

Two of the most well-known and successful experts in personal finance are Dave Ramsey and Robert Kiyosaki. Both have become incredibly wealthy following their approaches, sold millions of books sharing these strategies, and have an army of satisfied followers who have found financial success by applying what they learned.

Dave Ramsey is most well-known for his book *The Total Money Makeover* and his daily radio show/podcast. Robert Kiyosaki is most well-known for his book *Rich Dad Poor Dad*.

Each book goes into great detail on several strategies, and are recommended reading as you continue to learn more about personal finance.

Below, we will take a broad look at their approaches to debt, and how to handle it.

The Dave Ramsey Approach: Debt-Free Living

Dave Ramsey's philosophy is simple:

"If you live like no one else now, later you can live like no one else."

That is to say "If you live with an unusual level of discipline now to become debt free, you can live with much more financial comfort than most people later".

Ramsey teaches that **debt is dangerous** and should be avoided whenever possible. He often quotes Proverbs 22:7 from the bible, which says "the borrower is slave to the lender".

Proverbs 22:7

The borrower is slave to the lender

His method focuses on eliminating debt, saving for emergencies, and building wealth slowly and safely.

The Baby Steps

1. **Save $1,000 for a starter emergency fund.**
2. **Pay off all debt (except your home) using the Debt Snowball method.**
3. **Save 3–6 months of expenses for emergencies.**
4. **Invest 15% of income for retirement.**
5. **Save for children's education.**
6. **Pay off your home early.**
7. **Build wealth and give generously.**

Ramsey believes that peace of mind and freedom outweigh potential returns from "smart" borrowing. Debt, he says, removes options and creates stress; and most people don't manage it well.

Why It Works

- Simple, easy to follow, and emotionally motivating.
- Focuses on security and discipline.
- Encourages generosity once financial freedom is achieved.
- Resistant to market crashes.

- Barring major unexpected expenses (ex. legal or medical), following this approach will make you financially secure over time.

Potential Drawbacks

- Slower wealth-building potential.
- May be too conservative for some entrepreneurs or investors.
- Avoids nearly all forms of leverage; even responsible ones.

Ramsey's philosophy fits people who value **stability, low risk, and emotional peace** over aggressive growth.

Reflection Question:

- What kind of peace would being 100% debt-free bring you?

The Robert Kiyosaki Approach: Leveraging to Build Wealth

Robert Kiyosaki, author of *Rich Dad Poor Dad*, takes a nearly opposite stance. He teaches that **"the rich use debt to get richer."**

To him, the key isn't avoiding debt; it's learning to control it. Good debt can fund investments that produce income, while bad debt drains your resources.

His Core Ideas

- **Use leverage (borrowed money) to buy assets that make money:** (Examples: real estate, businesses, or investments that generate cash flow.)
- **Focus on financial education:** Know how money, taxes, and investing work before taking risks.
- **Understand cash flow:** An asset puts money in your pocket; a liability takes money out.

As a simple example, imagine that you had a $100,000 loan at 5% interest. Instead of paying it off quickly, you decide to invest it in a mutual fund that makes 12% annually.

By paying the minimal balance on the loan and keeping the rest in the mutual fund, you can pocket the difference between the mutual fund gains and the lower interest on the loan.

If used responsibly, Kiyosaki-style leverage can multiply opportunities, turning $10,000 into ownership of a $100,000 asset.

Why It Works

- Builds wealth faster when things go right.
- Encourages business thinking and financial literacy.
- Recognizes that inflation makes long-term fixed debt cheaper over time.

Potential Drawbacks

- Requires high discipline and skill.
- Involves real risk; leveraged investments can fail.
- Market crashes can put you at great risk of bankruptcy.
- Doesn't work well without strong cash flow management.

Kiyosaki's philosophy fits people who value **growth, opportunity, and strategic risk** over guaranteed safety.

Two Roads, One Destination

Neither Ramsey nor Kiyosaki is "right" for everyone. Ramsey focuses on peace, while Kiyosaki focuses on potential and maximizing how much money you can make.

The best approach depends on your **temperament, goals, and readiness.**

Mindset	Ramsey Style	Kiyosaki Style
Core Goal	Freedom from debt	Growth through leverage
View of Debt	Avoid it	Use it wisely
Focus	Security, simplicity	Opportunity, expansion
Personality Fit	Risk-averse, steady	Entrepreneurial, strategic
Main Risk	Growing slower	Losing control of debt

Some people start with Ramsey's safety net, then move toward Kiyosaki's strategy once they're educated and stable. Others never leave the debt-free path, and still build meaningful wealth through consistency.

Key Takeaways

1. **Debt isn't the enemy, ignorance is:** Whether you avoid or use debt, you must understand it deeply.
2. **Risk and reward are connected:** The more risk you take, the higher your potential reward, but also your potential loss.
3. **Peace of mind is priceless:** The right strategy is the one that lets you sleep soundly while moving toward your goals.
4. **You can mix approaches:** Pay off harmful debt first, then strategically use good debt for growth opportunities later.

Reflection Question:

- Which approach makes more sense for you? Why?

Activities: Two Ways to Handle Debt

1. Pay Off Debt Fast or Invest for Big Gains?

Imagine that you have an 8-year, $100,000 loan with a 6.5% interest rate. You can spend $2,500 a month to pay it off fast, or make the minimum payment ($1,338) and invest the rest ($1,162).

Compare how much money you would make or lose in each scenario. Stock #3 is filled in for reference. Assume that stock gain/loss is after capital gains taxes are taken out.

Investment	Stock Gain/Loss	Interest Paid	Interest Earned	Total Gain/Loss
Minimum Payment only	-	$28,507	-	-
Fast Payoff (3.83 years)	-	$13,008	-	+$15,499 vs. minimum
Stock #1	+15%	$28,507		
Stock #2	-5%	$28,507		
Stock #3	+8%	$28,507	$42,128	+$13,621

How would it feel if you invested in stock #1 instead of quickly paying off your debt?

___

___

___

___

___

How would it feel if you invested in stock #2 instead of quickly paying off your debt?

____

____

____

____

____

2. Financial Philosophy Journal Prompt

Write a short paragraph about which approach you think fits your personality best. Are you naturally cautious or ambitious with money? How might your answer change when you're older and earning more?

____

____

____

____

____

____

____

____

____

Part 5: Investing

Chapter 11: Why Invest?

Opening Story: The Two Savers

When Emma and Ben each got their first real jobs at age 18, both decided to save money every month.

Emma put $100 into a regular savings account earning about 1%.

Ben decided to learn about investing and started putting his $100 into a low-cost index fund that averaged about 8% per year.

At first, their balances looked almost the same. After five years, Emma had saved about $6,100. Ben had about $7,400.

But after twenty years? Emma had around **$24,000.** Ben had over **$58,000.**

Neither worked harder. They simply used money differently.
That's the power of investing: **your money starts working while you sleep.**

Saving vs. Investing

Saving and investing both involve setting money aside, but they serve different purposes.

Although investing often grows money much faster than saving, it also has more risk. Picking the wrong securities or buying at the wrong time can make your money shrink.

Saving	Investing
Short-term (1–5 years)	Long-term (5+ years)
Safe, predictable	Can grow faster but has risk
Keeps money available	Usually locks money for growth
Best for emergencies or near goals	Best for building wealth and beating inflation

You save to protect money. You invest to grow money.

If saving is like parking your car safely in a garage, investing is like sending it on a long, productive road trip that returns with more passengers.

Reflection Question:

- Which do you think you're more comfortable with right now? Saving or investing?

How Compounding Works

Compounding is the "magic of money." It's what happens when your investments earn profits, and then those profits start earning more profits.

Here's an example:

- Year 1: You invest $100 and earn 10%. You now have $110.
- Year 2: You earn 10% again, but now it's on $110, not just $100. You earn $11 instead of $10.
- Over time, the effect snowballs; your money grows faster and faster without extra effort.

Albert Einstein supposedly called compound interest "the eighth wonder of the world." Whether or not he really said that, the idea holds: **time and consistency matter more than luck or timing.**

The Power of Time

Let's see how starting early makes a huge difference. Imagine that you invest $100 per month, earning 7% per year.

Years Invested	Total You Put In	Total at 7% Growth
10	$12,000	$17,300
20	$24,000	$52,000
30	$36,000	**$118,000**

That's over **$80,000 more** simply from starting early and letting compounding work. The secret ingredient isn't timing the market, it's **time in** the market.

Your Money Works While You Sleep

When you invest, your dollars become tiny workers. They're out there 24/7, earning dividends, growing in value, and compounding returns.

You don't need to constantly watch or worry over them; you just need to keep sending new workers out to join the team.

Of course, just like workers, investments need guidance:

- Diversify (don't put all your money in one company or asset).
- Stay patient (markets go up and down, but long-term growth wins).
- Reinvest your earnings (that's how compounding accelerates).

Risk and Reward

Investing always involves **risk**; the chance your investment might go down in value. But not investing also has a risk: **inflation**.

If prices rise 3% every year and your savings only earn 1%, your money slowly loses buying power. Even if your savings earn 3%, you're still not gaining buying power.

Think of it like this:

- Keeping money in savings protects it from loss.
- Investing protects it from *being left behind.*

Different types of investments have different levels of risk and reward:

Type	Risk Level	Potential Reward	Example
Savings Account	Very Low	Very Low	HYSA, CDs
Bonds	Low to Moderate	Moderate	Government or corporate bonds
Alternative Assets	Moderate to High	Moderate to High	Gold, Bitcoin
Index Funds	Moderate	High	S&P 500, total market ETFs
Individual Stocks	High	Very High	Owning shares in one company

The key is balance; some safe, some growing. We will learn more about these specific investments in the next chapter.

Reflection Question:

- Which investment types interest you most? Which do you feel least comfortable with?

Investing for Real Goals

You can invest for anything important to your future:

- College or career training
- A car or down payment
- Retirement or financial independence
- Starting a business someday

Make sure that you know when you will need the money. If you are looking to save for a car that you want to buy next year, investing risks short term losses that slow you down.

If you are looking to save money for a business you want to start in ten years, the odds are in your favor that investing will be more fruitful than saving.

The earlier you start, the more powerful your investments become. Even small, regular contributions make a difference.

The Emotional Side of Investing

Investing isn't just math, it's mindset. It teaches patience, consistency, and resilience.

When the market drops, many people panic and sell. Smart investors remember: dips are normal; time heals volatility.

The broad goal of investing is to buy low and sell high. When the market is down, opportunistic investors see an opportunity to buy low, as if the market were "on sale".

Staying calm and consistent is one of the hardest and most rewarding skills to master.

Reflection Questions:

- What would future-you thank you for investing in today?
- How would you feel if you invested $100 in a stock that dropped to $90? Would you be tempted to sell it before it drops lower? Would you be tempted to buy more at the lower price?

Tips for Getting Started

1. **Learn Before You Leap:** Understand what you're investing in. Don't just chase "hot tips."
2. **Start Small:** Even a few dollars a week builds the habit.
3. **Automate It:** Schedule recurring transfers to your investment account.
4. **Diversify:** Use index funds or ETFs to spread risk across hundreds of companies.
5. **Stay In It for the Long Haul:** Investing isn't about getting rich quick; it's about staying invested through ups and downs.

Chapter 11 Reflection Questions

1. How is investing different from saving?
2. Why does compounding make time more valuable than timing?

Activities: Why Invest?

1. Compound Growth Visual

Chart how $150 a month could grow at 7% over 10, 20, and 30 years. Start with your current age or when you plan to start investing.

For "Ending Age", write in the age you plan to begin withdrawing money and calculate your totals. For example, if you start at 18 and plan to retire at 65, you will calculate dollars invested and growth on 47 years.

Years Invested	Total Dollars Invested	Total at 7% Growth
Starting Age:	$0	$0
10 years	$18,000	
20 years	$36,000	
30 years	$54,000	
Ending Age:		

2. Future-You Letter

Write a short letter to your future self (10–20 years from now). Thank yourself for starting to save and invest early. Describe one thing you hope those choices allow you to do or experience.

____

____

____

____

____

____

____

____

Chapter 12: Common Investment Options

Opening Story: The Egg Lesson

When Sofia's grandma taught her how to cook, she said, "Never carry all the eggs in one basket." Sofia didn't understand until the next morning, when she tripped on the kitchen rug and dropped the basket. Scrambled breakfast, indeed.

Later, when her older brother was learning about investing, he said, "That's exactly what diversification means. If one stock or investment cracks, you don't lose everything."

Grandma's kitchen wisdom turned out to be *financial wisdom* too.

Why There Are So Many Investment Options

No single investment works for everyone or every goal. Each one has its own mix of **risk**, **reward**, and **purpose**; like different tools in a toolbox.

A hammer can't do a screwdriver's job, and a savings account can't grow like an index fund. Smart investors learn what each "tool" does and use the right one for the right situation.

Let's review six common investment options. Specific investment options will be included as real-world examples, but **<u>their inclusion is not a recommendation to invest in them</u>**.

1. Stocks: Owning Pieces of Companies

When you buy a stock, you're buying a small piece of a company. If that company grows and earns profits, your share becomes more valuable. Some companies also pay **dividends**, which are small payments to shareholders.

Stocks are the engine of most long-term portfolios because they historically offer the highest returns over time. But they also go up and down the most.

Example: If you had invested $1,500 in Walmart in 2000, it would be worth around $10,200 today, plus dividends paid. That's the long-term power of ownership.

Risk Level: Moderate to High
Best For: Long-term goals (10+ years)
Tip: Diversify! Don't buy one company. It is exciting to look at companies that experience rapid growth, but there is also risk of investing in a company that goes out of business.

2. Bonds: Lending, Not Owning

Bonds are the opposite of stocks. When you buy a bond, you're **lending** money to a company or government, and they promise to pay you back later with interest.

They don't grow as fast as stocks, but they're more stable. If stocks are the gas pedal of investing, bonds are the brake pedal; they help steady your ride.

Example: A ten-year United States Treasury bond purchased in September 2025 would have a 4% yield (average annual return).

Risk Level: Low to Moderate
Best For: Medium-term goals (3–10 years) or balancing portfolios
Examples: U.S. Treasury Bonds, municipal bonds, or corporate bonds

3. ETFs and Mutual Funds: The Easy Mix

ETFs (Exchange-Traded Funds) and mutual funds are like **investment bundles**. Instead of buying one company's stock, you buy a fund that includes many different stocks or bonds. That way, one company's bad day doesn't ruin your results.

They make diversification simple, even with small amounts of money.

Top 10 Holdings AS OF 09/30/2025 More >

38.84% of Total Portfolio

507 holdings as of 09/30/2025 | 502 issuers as of 09/30/2025

NVDA	NVIDIA CORP	7.97%
MSFT	MICROSOFT CORP	6.74%
AAPL	APPLE INC	6.62%
AMZN	AMAZON.COM INC	3.73%
META	META PLATFORMS INC CL A	2.79%
AVGO	BROADCOM INC	2.72%
GOOGL	ALPHABET INC CL A	2.48%
TSLA	TESLA INC	2.19%
GOOG	ALPHABET INC CL C	1.99%
BRK/B	BERKSHIRE HATHAWAY INC CL B	1.61%

$FXAIX Asset Allocation

ETFs and mutual funds can be broad or narrow. Some funds have exposure all publicly traded companies (total market fund), while others can be specific to investment types (large cap, high dividend, growth, value) or sectors (technology, energy, military).

Case Study: FXAIX (Fidelity 500 Index Fund)
FXAIX is one of many funds that tracks the S&P 500; a collection of the 500 biggest U.S. companies. Over the past 30 years, it has averaged roughly 8–10% per year.

That means if you invested $100 monthly since the early 1990s, it could now be worth over $150,000.

Risk Level: Moderate
Best For: Beginners, long-term savers, or anyone wanting broad exposure
Tip: Look at the expense ratio and dividend rate to get a better feel for how strong an ETF or mutual fund is. If choosing between two options that both average 10% per year, the one with a lower expense ratio and higher dividends is the stronger option.

4. Real Estate: Property as an Investment

Buying property, whether a home, rental unit, or land, can be a powerful way to build wealth. Real estate often rises in value over time and can also produce income through rent.

However, it requires more money upfront and ongoing maintenance. Property taxes can add up too.

It's less "liquid" than stocks, meaning it's harder to sell quickly.

Risk Level: Moderate
Best For: Adults with stable income, long-term investors

Tip: Real estate can be "hands-on" (you own property) or "hands-off" through Real Estate Investment Trusts (REITs) that you can buy like stocks.

5. Cryptocurrency: Digital Money and Speculation

Cryptocurrencies like Bitcoin and Ethereum are **digital assets** built on blockchain technology. They can rise or fall in value dramatically because they're driven by supply, demand, and belief rather than profits or earnings.

Some investors see them as the *future of money*; others see them as *risky speculation.*

It's best to treat crypto as a small "extra" investment, not a main one.

As a new technology, cryptocurrencies have had a mix of extreme success (Bitcoin, Ethereum, Solana) and extreme failure, with many cryptocurrencies being created with the intention to scam investors. The common term for this is a "rug pull".

Risk Level: Very High
Best For: Experienced investors willing to take risk
Tip: Never invest more in crypto than you can afford to lose. There may come a time when major countries seek to ban it to protect their paper currency (worth less), or they may decide it's the future and invest in it heavily (worth more). Policy can change as quickly as politicians change.

6. Precious Metals: Gold and Silver

Gold and silver have been valuable for thousands of years because they're rare and can't be printed like money. They also have industrial use in many modern items. People often buy precious metals during times of inflation or uncertainty.

They don't earn interest or dividends, but they can hold value when markets drop. Think of them as a **store of value** or insurance policy, not a growth engine.

Risk Level: Moderate (price swings, no yield)
Best For: Diversifying or protecting purchasing power
Tip: Keep metals to a small percentage of your portfolio (5–10%) if you choose to include them.

Diversification: Don't Put All Your Eggs in One Basket

Diversification simply means spreading your money around. That way, if one type of investment goes down, others may hold steady or go up.

For example:

- Stocks might drop in a recession.
- Bonds often stay steady or rise when stocks fall.
- Real estate and gold sometimes move differently from other assets.

A **balanced portfolio** mixes several asset types based on your risk tolerance and goals. Below is a sample balanced portfolio.

Asset Type	Percentage	Purpose
Stocks / ETFs	60%	Growth
Bonds	25%	Stability
Real Estate / REITs	10%	Income & inflation protection
Precious Metals / Crypto	5%	Diversification & optional risk

This is just one example. Younger investors might take more risk with 80% stocks; retirees might prefer more bonds for safety.

Risk Tolerance and Time Horizon

Every investor is different. Two people could own the same portfolio but feel completely opposite emotions when the market drops 10%.

Risk Tolerance

Risk tolerance is your comfort level with ups and downs. If you lose sleep when values dip, you may want to keep more in safer assets like bonds and savings.

If you see a drop in values as a time to buy in at a low price, riskier assets may work better for you. You can handle difficult times without selling off good long-term assets in a panic.

Time Horizon

Time Horizon is how long you plan to invest before needing the money.

- **Short-term (1–5 years):** Focus on safety and liquidity.
- **Medium-term (5–10 years):** Mix growth and stability.
- **Long-term (10+ years):** Lean toward growth (stocks, ETFs, real estate).

The longer your time horizon, the more risk you can afford, because you have time for the market to recover.

Chapter 12 Reflection Questions

1. Why do you think investors own more than one kind of investment?
2. Which investment option seems most interesting to you? Why?
3. How does time affect how much risk you can take?
4. What would you include in your own "balanced basket"?

Activities: Common Investment Options

1. Build Your Own Investment Mix

Create a pie chart showing how you might divide a $1,000 investment among different asset types. Label each slice with both the percentage and the purpose (growth, safety, diversification).

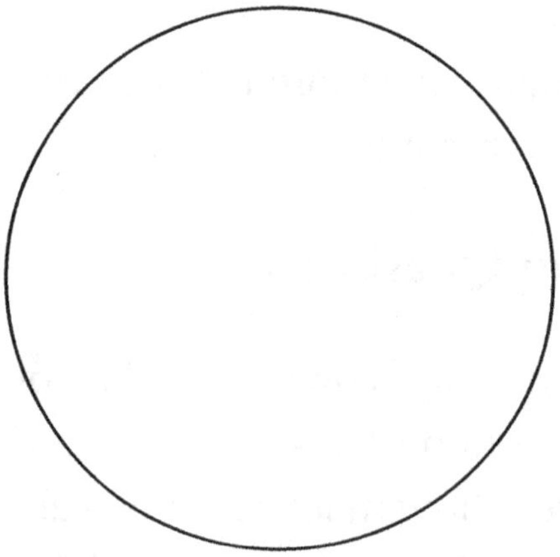

2. Stocks or Index Funds?

Imagine that it's October of 2024, and you have been closely following the upcoming election. You are confident that Donald Trump will win, and you strongly believe that he will spend a lot of taxpayer money on military equipment for the US and allied countries.

Time will prove you are correct, but how much money did you make on this prediction? That depends on whether you invested in the right defense companies, an index fund covering defense companies, or the wrong defense companies.

Fill out the table below with 1 year returns on $1,000 invested in each of these companies and index funds in this sector.

Stock or ETF	OCT 2024 Price	OCT 2025 Price	% Gain or Loss	Value of $1,000 investment
$PLTR	$43	$175		$
$GE	$191	$291		$
$SHLD	$38	$68		$
$ITA	$150	$206		$
$GD	$302	$333		$
$LMT	$610	$505		$

$PLTR = Palantir (company stock)
$GE = GE Aerospace (company stock)
$SHLD = Global X Defense Tech ETF
$ITA = iShares U.S. Aerospace & Defense ETF
$GD = General Dynamics Corp (company stock)
$LMT = Lockheed Martin Corp (company stock)

1. If you had $6,000 to invest and put it all in Lockheed Martin, how would you feel?

____

____

2. If you had $6,000 to invest and split it equally among these six options, how much would you have after one year?

____

____

____

3. If you knew that some companies would have explosive growth and others would decline, would you rather try to pick the winners like Palantir for the biggest reward, or an ETF for a safer but smaller reward?

____

____

____

Chapter 13: Investing for the Long Haul

Opening Story: The Two Choices

Griffin's grandpa gave him a choice on his 13th birthday:

"You can have $1,000 now, or I'll give you $5,000 when you turn 21."

Griffin hesitated. Eight years felt like forever. He could buy a new phone right now, or wait almost a decade for more money than he'd ever had before.

After thinking it over, he chose the second option. When his 21st birthday came, Grandpa smiled and said, "I'm proud of you. You didn't just earn more money, you learned how to think like an investor."

That's what long-term investing is about: trading short-term excitement for lasting rewards.

Avoiding Get-Rich-Quick Traps

The internet is full of promises: "Turn $100 into $10,000 in a week!" or "This one secret stock will make you rich!"

These traps prey on impatience and fear of missing out (FOMO). But real investors know that **slow and steady wins every time.**

How to Spot a Scam or a Trap

- **Guaranteed high returns**: No real investment is 100% safe and fast-growing.
- **Pressure to act now**: If you're being rushed, it's probably a bad deal.
- **Too complex to explain simply**: If you don't understand how it works, don't invest in it.

The truth? Wealth grows like a tree; gradually, quietly, and only with time and care.

Reflection Question:

- Would you rather have $1,000 now or $5,000 later? Why?

Staying Calm Through Market Ups and Downs

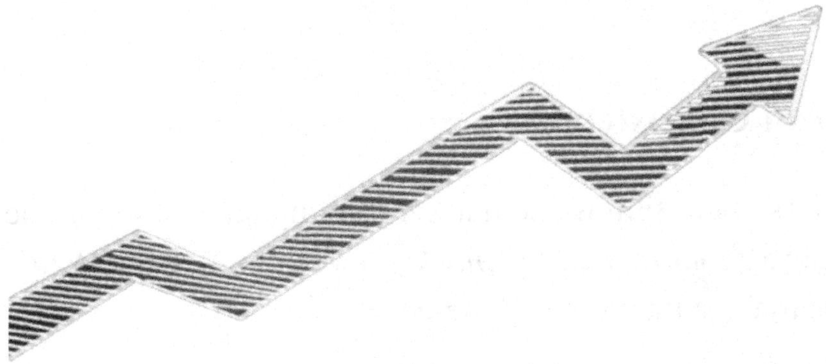

The stock market is like a roller coaster. It goes up, it dips down, it climbs again. But here's the secret: you only lose money if you jump off the ride too soon.

If you bought a stock for $50 and it is now $40, you have not lost $10 until you sell the stock. If that stock rebounds up to $60 and you never sold it, you are now up $10 on paper.

In the short term, the market can look wild. In the long term, it has always trended upward to this point. That's why long-term investors focus on **decades, not days.**

The Emotional Cycle of Investing

1. **Optimism:** "This is exciting!"
2. **Doubt:** "Why is my account lower?"
3. **Fear:** "Should I sell before I lose more?"
4. **Patience:** "I'll stay invested."
5. **Relief:** "The market recovered."
6. **Confidence:** "I'm glad I stayed in."

If you keep emotions in check and stick to your plan, you are in a strong position to win.

Tip: Checking your investments less often actually makes most people better investors!

The Power of Consistency

Investing is less about timing the market (buying and selling at the perfect times) and more about *time in the market.* Even small, consistent contributions make a massive difference.

Example:

If you invest $50 a month for 30 years at 7%, you'll end up with nearly **$60,000.**

But if you skip the first 10 years and start investing $75 a month year 11, you'll only have **$38,000** even though you invested the same total amount!

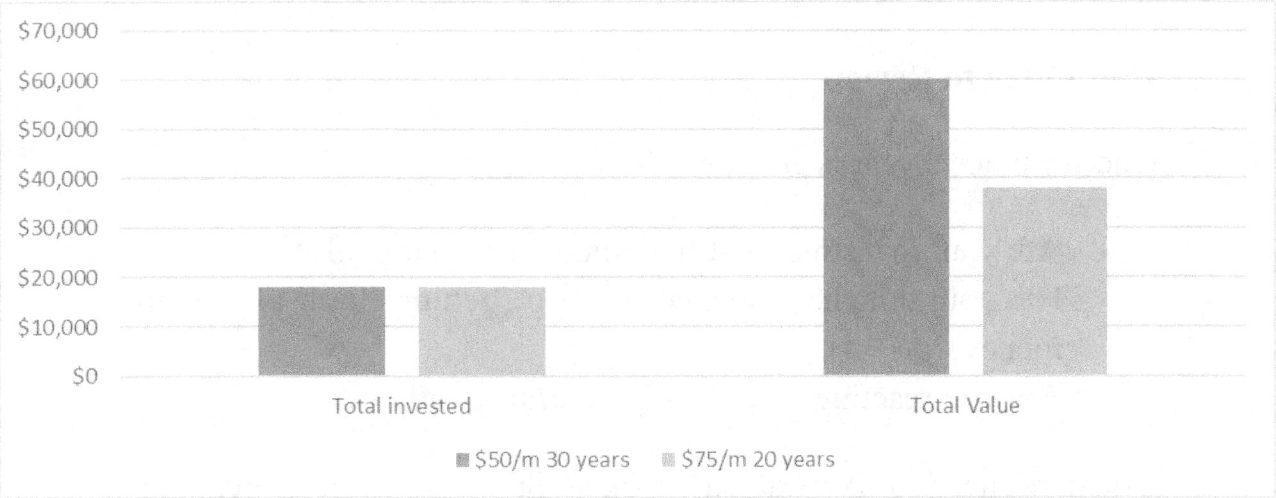

The difference here isn't money, it's *time.*

Consistency beats intensity

Rebalancing and Reviewing

As your investments grow, some categories will outpace others. That's good, but it can throw your portfolio off balance.

Rebalancing

Rebalancing means adjusting your investments to keep your preferred mix of stocks, bonds, and other assets.

Example:

- You start with 60% stocks and 40% bonds.
- After a few years, stocks rise and now make up 70% of your portfolio.
- You sell a little stock and buy more bonds to restore the 60/40 balance.

It's like keeping your car aligned; it ensures smoother travel.

How Often to Review

Once or twice a year is enough. Check:

- Are your investments still aligned with your goals?
- Has your time horizon changed (e.g., getting closer to needing the money)?
- Are you reacting emotionally or strategically?

You don't need to fix what isn't broken. Small adjustments beat big overhauls.

Building Habits Early

The best investors aren't necessarily the smartest, they're the most consistent. Good investment habits like consistency are easiest to build when you're young.

Simple Ways to Practice Now

1. **Mock Portfolios:** Create a pretend investment account using free online tools or apps (ex. Yahoo Finance). Track how your "investments" perform over a few months.

2. **Savings and Investing Apps:** Many banks and apps let you invest spare change automatically. Every little bit adds up.
3. **Follow the News (but don't panic):** Learn to read financial headlines critically. Ask, "Is this long-term news or short-term noise?"
4. **Talk About Money:** Ask family members how they invest, what mistakes they've made, and what they've learned.
5. **Think in Decades, Not Days:** Every investment choice should support your future self; 10, 20, or 30 years from now.

The Magic of Patience

Imagine planting an apple tree. You water it every week, but it takes years before it bears fruit. You don't dig it up every few days to check the roots; you trust the process.

That's investing.

It's about faith in long-term growth. Markets may fall, but they've always risen again. Patience, not prediction, is the real superpower of long-term wealth builders.

Reflection Question:

- How might your life be different 20 years from now if you started investing today?

The Rule of 72

Here's a fun math trick to show how compounding works:
Divide **72 by your interest rate** to estimate how many years it takes for money to double.

Interest Rate	Years to Double
4%	18 years
6%	12 years
8%	9 years
10%	7 years

If you invest $1,000 at 8%, it doubles roughly every 9 years:
$1,000 → $2,000 → $4,000 → $8,000 → $16,000 in 36 years!
That's why long-term investing works best when you start early.

Chapter 13 Reflection Questions

1. Why do get-rich-quick promises usually fail?
2. How can patience protect you from poor investing decisions?
3. What does rebalancing mean, and why is it important?

Activities: Investing for the Long Haul

1. Create a Pretend Investment Tracker

Make a mock portfolio of five investments (stocks, ETFs, alternative assets, precious metals, etc.). Track their performance for one month.

Notice how prices move, and practice staying calm through ups and downs.

Investment Name	Starting Value	Current Value	% Change

After 30 days, write a short reflection. What surprised you about watching investments over time?

____

____

____

____

____

2. 7-Day "Grow Your Knowledge" Investing Challenge

Each day for a week, learn one small thing about investing.
Ideas include:

- Watch a short educational video
- Read a news article about the stock market
- Ask a parent what they invest in

- Look up a company's stock price history
- Learn a new financial term (like "dividend" or "index fund")

At the end of the challenge, list **three things you understand now** that you didn't before.

#1:

____

____

#2:

____

____

#3:

____

____

3. The Long-Term Vision Board

Using a posterboard or blank piece of paper, cut out or draw images of what you'd like your future to include (ex. college, travel, home, business). Write how investing could help make each goal possible.

Keep it where you'll see it often, as it's a reminder of what you're working toward.

Part 6: Habits & Mindset

Chapter 14: Financial Habits That Stick

Opening Story: The Power of Small Things

Every morning before school, Sydney's mom asked the same question:

"Did you pack your lunch?"

It sounded simple, even annoying at times. But over the years, those packed lunches saved hundreds of dollars and taught Sydney something bigger; small habits matter.

Just like brushing your teeth keeps your mouth healthy, good money habits keep your finances healthy. They don't require big changes or huge sacrifices, just consistency. When small actions repeat long enough, they become unstoppable momentum.

That's what we call **The Flywheel of Good Habits.**

The Flywheel of Good Habits

A *flywheel* is a heavy wheel used in engines that stores energy. At first, it's hard to push. But once it's spinning, it stays in motion with very little effort.

Financial habits work the same way:

1. You start small.
2. It feels slow.
3. But each step builds momentum.
4. Soon, progress becomes automatic.

Imagine a circle divided into four stages:

- **Track → Plan → Act → Review → (Back to Track).**

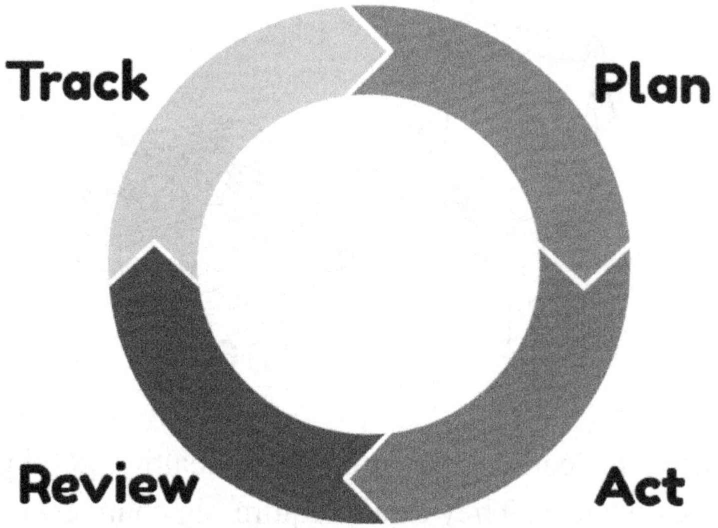

Each part feeds the next, turning financial awareness into long-term progress.

Daily, Weekly, Monthly Habits

The key to financial success isn't doing something huge once, it's doing small things regularly.

Daily Habits

- **Track your spending:** Write down what you buy or use an app. Awareness is step one.
- **Pause before purchases:** Ask: "Do I need this, or do I just want it?"
- **Save automatically:** Even small daily transfers add up fast.

Weekly Habits

- **Review your budget:** Did you stay within your plan? Adjust if needed.
- **Plan upcoming expenses:** Birthdays, gas, groceries; predict what's ahead.
- **Talk about money:** Check in with family about goals or new ideas.

Monthly Habits

- **Update your savings and investment progress:** Celebrate every milestone.
- **Pay bills on time:** Automation helps avoid late fees and stress.
- **Reflect and reset:** What went well this month? What will you improve next month?

Consistency turns these routines into reflexes. You won't have to think about them, they'll just happen.

Reflection Question:

- Which financial habit could you start this week?

Avoiding Lifestyle Creep

"Lifestyle creep" happens when your spending rises as your income rises. You earn more, but somehow there's still nothing left at the end of the month.

It often starts with small upgrades: a better phone, a pricier coffee, a new streaming service. None are bad on their own, but they quietly increase your monthly baseline.

How to Prevent Lifestyle Creep

1. **Set a Savings Percentage:** Save or invest a fixed portion (like 20%) of every raise or gift.
2. **Upgrade Mindfully:** Ask, "Will this purchase make my life meaningfully better, or just temporarily exciting?"
3. **Avoid Comparing:** Someone will *always* have more. Focus on your own progress.
4. **Revisit Goals:** More money should mean more opportunity, not more clutter.

Living below your means doesn't mean living without joy, it means leaving room for future freedom.

Emotional Spending

Money and emotions are deeply connected. People spend when they're sad, bored, stressed, or even happy. Advertisers know this, and use it to their advantage.

Before spending emotionally, try this:

- Pause and take a breath.
- Ask: "What am I really feeling right now?"
- Wait 24 hours before buying anything over a set amount (say, $50).

Most "needs" disappear with time. Buying things for emotional comfort rarely fixes the real problem, but saving or giving often feels genuinely good.

Tracking Net Worth Over Time

Net worth isn't a bragging number, it's your financial progress report. It shows how all your habits are adding up.

Net Worth = What You Own – What You Owe

Example:

Assets (What You Own)	Value
Savings Account	$1,000
Car	$5,000
Investments	$2,000
Total Assets	**$8,000**
Liabilities (What You Owe)	**Amount**
Credit Card	$500
Car Loan	$2,000
Total Liabilities	**$2,500**

Net Worth = $8,000 – $2,500 = $5,500

The goal isn't perfection, it's progress. When your net worth grows each year, it means your habits are working.

Track it once every few months. Watching the number rise is motivating, and it helps you stay focused long after the excitement of a new goal fades.

Planning Ahead

Being proactive turns surprises into simple adjustments. Financially confident people don't just react, they *anticipate.*

Ways to plan ahead:

- Keep a list of upcoming events and costs.
- Save for big yearly expenses like holidays or school supplies in advance.
- Set reminders for bill due dates, renewals, and subscriptions.
- Review your budget at the start of each new month.

Planning builds calm into your finances. You'll still face surprises, but they won't feel like emergencies.

Reflection Questions

1. Which financial habit could you start this week, and why?
2. What daily or weekly habit would make the biggest difference for your money?
3. How does tracking your spending or net worth help you stay motivated?
4. How can you prevent "lifestyle creep" as your income grows?

Activities: Financial Habits That Stick

1. Habit Tracker Printable

Create a habit tracker for the month. List 3–5 small financial habits you want to build.

Examples:

- Record my spending every day.
- Transfer $5 to savings each week.
- Review my budget every Sunday.

Each time you complete a habit, mark a check or color a box. By the end of the month, look for streaks; those are your flywheel starting to spin.

Habit Description	Week 1	Week 2	Week 3	Week 4
#1:				
#2:				
#3:				
#4:				
#5:				

2. "The $10 Challenge"

Pick a goal (saving, giving, or investing) and find creative ways to come up with $10 each week for it. Ideas might include selling unused items, skipping one treat, or doing a small chore for someone else. Track progress for four weeks to show how tiny efforts add up quickly.

Reflect on this exercise here:

____

____

____

____

____

3. "Future Cost Forecast"

Choose one habit or expense (like daily coffee, streaming services, or in-game purchases). Calculate how much it costs over a year, and how much that same amount could grow if saved or invested instead.

Habit: ____

How much it costs per year: ______________________________________

How much it could grow if saved or invested:

____

____

Reflect on whether that habit feels worth it long-term. Do you want to scale back on that habit and invest the difference?

____

____

____

____

____

____

Chapter 15: The Power of Giving

Opening Story: The Pizza Fund

When Emma's soccer team learned that their coach's car had broken down, they decided to help. They could have shrugged and moved on, but instead, one teammate suggested, "What if we all chipped in a few dollars?"

By the end of practice, they had enough to buy their coach a week's worth of bus passes and a gift card for auto parts. It didn't fix the car, but it fixed something bigger; the feeling that they were all in it together.

That's the power of giving: small actions that create huge ripples.

Why Giving Belongs in Every Financial Plan

Many people think of giving as something you do after you've achieved success. But wise givers understand that giving is part of success itself.

When you share what you have, whether it's time, money, or skills, you strengthen both your community and your own mindset. Giving teaches gratitude, perspective, and purpose. It reminds you that money isn't just for spending, but also for creating impact.

Even businesses recognize this. Companies that give to charity often have happier employees and more loyal customers. Generosity changes how people feel about what they do and how they see one another.

The Paradox of Giving: You Gain by Letting Go

It may sound strange, but giving doesn't actually reduce your wealth; it multiplies it in other ways. When you give, you build stronger relationships, feel more fulfilled and grateful, and often inspire others to do the same.

Research shows that people who give regularly report higher happiness levels than those who don't. Generosity releases "feel-good" hormones that last much longer than the thrill of a new purchase. The return on giving isn't measured in dollars but in joy, connection, and meaning.

The Three T's: Time, Talent, and Treasure

Everyone has something to give, no matter their age or income. That's where the Three T's come in.

Time is the first T. When you volunteer, help neighbors, or simply listen to someone who needs support, you give something priceless; your presence. You might visit a nursing home, help at a local food pantry, or organize a park cleanup. Giving your time shows others they matter.

Talent is the second T. Sharing your skills can help more people than you realize. If you're good at drawing, make cards for a hospital. If you know your way around technology, help a community group with their website. Talents grow when they're shared.

Treasure is the third T. This refers to giving money or resources. It doesn't have to be large; five dollars can make a real difference when given thoughtfully. The key is intention: giving because you want to help, not because you have to.

How Giving Strengthens Financial Skills

Generosity also improves financial literacy.

Budgeting for giving teaches discipline.

Researching charities develops critical thinking.

Tracking the impact of your donations builds accountability.

In a way, generosity is like strength training for your financial muscles; it keeps you aware, flexible, and grounded.

Integrating Giving into Everyday Life

Think of giving as a habit, not a one-time act. It can become part of your daily rhythm. Some people follow the "10% Rule," choosing to give a tenth of their income or allowance to causes they care about. Others use "round-up giving," donating spare change from everyday purchases.

Families can make it fun with a giving jar, where everyone contributes coins each week and votes on where to send the money. You can also celebrate birthdays by giving to a cause instead of receiving gifts, or share your talents by teaching or helping others in your community.

When generosity becomes part of life, it changes how you see money; not as something to keep, but as something that flows through you to others.

The Ripple Effect of Generosity

Every act of giving starts a chain reaction. When you help one person, they often pay it forward, and soon you've changed more lives than you could ever count.

It's like dropping a pebble into water. The ripples spread far beyond where it lands. You might never see how far your kindness reaches, but the impact continues, touching people in ways you can't imagine. Generosity doesn't just change the world around you; it changes you.

Chapter 15 Reflection Questions:

1. If you could give $100 away, where would you give it and why?
2. What's one skill or talent you could share to help others?
3. How could your family make giving a regular part of your budget or routine?
4. How does giving make you feel compared to spending on yourself?

Activities: The Power of Giving

1. Family Giving Challenge

As a family, choose one cause you care about, such as animals, the environment, or hunger relief. Set a small goal for how much you'd like to give this month, then decide how to raise it. You could save spare change, skip a treat each week, or host a mini fundraiser. At the end of the month, donate your total and reflect on what you learned.

Cause: ____

Fundraising goal: ________________________________

How will you raise it?

____

____

____

Reflection on what you learned:

____

____

____

____

2. The "Three T's" Planner Page

Use this chart to plan one act of giving in each category this month. Then, reflect on how each experience made you feel.

Type of Giving	Act of Giving	Date Completed	How It Felt
Time			
Talent			
Treasure			

3. Generosity Brainstorm

Make a list of five more creative ways to give that don't involve money. You could help a friend study, leave a kind note, donate books, or share your art online. Circle the one you'd like to try first.

1.____

2.____

3.____

4.____

5.____

Closing Thought

True wealth isn't just measured by what you keep, it's also measured by what you give. Generosity doesn't take away from your success; it defines it. When you use your money, time, and talents to help others, you make your community (and your own life) richer in every way.

If the topic of giving interests you and you want to take a deeper dive into it, check out *The Power of Giving* from this Life Skills Lab series.

Chapter 16: Building Your Financial Future

Opening Story: The Garden Grows

When Mateo was twelve, he started a tiny vegetable garden in his backyard. The first year, half his plants died. The next year, he learned about soil and sunlight, and his garden doubled in size. By the third year, he was selling cucumbers and tomatoes at the local farmers' market, and saving the profits for college.

One afternoon, his mom said, "You know, you're not just growing food. You're growing your future."

Building a financial life is a lot like that garden. You start small. You learn from your mistakes. And over time, your effort begins to multiply into something lasting.

Bringing It All Together

Throughout this book, you've explored how money flows through your life. You've learned how to earn it, manage it, grow it, and give it. Now it's time to put those lessons together into a picture of your financial future.

Each part supports the next. Earning gives you resources. Managing gives you control. Investing gives you growth. Giving gives you purpose. When all four work together, you build not just wealth, but *wisdom.*

Financial success isn't about being rich, it's about being ready. Ready for opportunities, ready for challenges, and ready to use money as a tool for good.

Three Time Frames: Short, Medium, and Long-Term Goals

Money goals come in different sizes, just like your dreams. Breaking them into short, medium, and long-term goals helps you stay focused and motivated.

Short-Term Goals

These are the things you want to achieve within a year. They're usually simple, concrete, and quick to measure.

Examples include saving for a new bike, earning enough to buy a laptop, or keeping a three-month emergency fund.

Short-term goals teach discipline and help you experience quick wins.

Saving is the ideal way to work towards these goals, as short-term market losses can disrupt your plans.

Medium-Term Goals

These take one to five years. They require planning, patience, and steady progress.

Saving for college, buying your first car, or building a small business all fit here.
These goals build habits, including budgeting, saving, and learning to delay gratification.

A mix of saving and investing is ideal to help you reach these goals. Savings accounts help keep you protected from market crashes, while exposure to the market gives you an opportunity for quicker growth if the market performs as it normally does.

Long-Term Goals

These are the big ones, taking five years or more. They might include buying a home, achieving financial independence, or retiring comfortably.

The key is consistency. Time turns small, repeated actions into life-changing results.

Investing is the best way to work toward long term goals, as the time it takes to reach them gives your investments time to rebound from any short-term losses.

Reflection Question:

- Which type of goal do you find easiest to plan for? Short, medium, or long-term?

How to Create a Financial Roadmap

A roadmap helps you move from dreaming to doing. It doesn't have to be complicated; it just needs to be clear.

1. **Start with your values.** What matters most to you? Freedom, security, creativity, generosity?
2. **Define specific goals.** Write them down in detail: what you want, how much it will cost, and when you want to achieve it.
3. **Break it into steps.** If your goal is to save $600 for a new laptop in six months, that means saving $100 a month.
4. **Track your progress.** Review your goals regularly and celebrate milestones.
5. **Adjust as life changes.** Your goals can evolve. Flexibility keeps you growing in the right direction.

A financial roadmap is personal. It should fit your dreams, not someone else's expectations.

The Habit Loop That Builds the Future

Your financial habits today shape who you'll be tomorrow. Saving a few dollars, resisting an impulse buy, or learning about investing might not seem like much right now. But together, they create momentum that compounds just like interest.

Try thinking of your habits as a loop:

1. **Cue:** Something reminds you to act (for example, payday).
2. **Action:** You move money into savings or investments.
3. **Reward:** You feel proud, confident, and in control.

Repeat that loop enough times, and it becomes automatic. You won't have to force yourself; you'll simply *become* someone who makes smart financial decisions naturally.

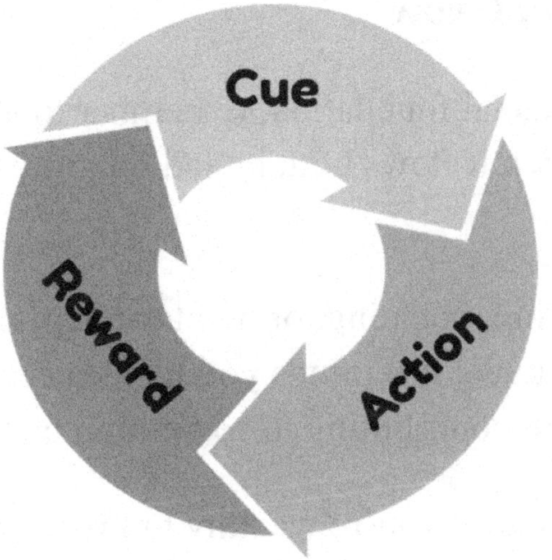

Continuous Learning and Adaptation

The world of money never stands still. New technology, markets, and opportunities appear all the time. What matters most is your willingness to learn.

Read about personal finance, ask questions, and pay attention to how the people you admire handle money. Try things on a small scale first, whether that's investing, budgeting, or starting a side business. When something doesn't work, treat it like feedback, not failure.

There are many people who have taken different paths to wealth and financial security, as illustrated with Dave Ramsey and Robert Kiyosaki earlier. Take the opportunity to read different personal finance books and understand different approaches. Notice what they all have in common, and see which case is most persuasive when they disagree.

Every mistake is a lesson. Every success is a building block. Financial wisdom comes from staying curious.

Giving Back as You Grow

As you build your financial foundation, remember to look outward. Money is most meaningful when it flows both in and out, meeting your needs and helping others.

Whether it's volunteering, donating, or mentoring, giving back keeps your goals grounded in gratitude. It reminds you that success isn't only about personal gain, it's about contributing to something bigger.

You don't have to wait until you're wealthy to give. You can give time, share knowledge, or simply make someone's day better. When you help others grow, your own success feels richer.

Closing Story: A Future Rewritten

At seventeen, Lila was worried about money. Her family lived paycheck to paycheck, and she didn't think things could ever change. But one day, her teacher introduced a lesson on budgeting and investing.

Something clicked. Lila began tracking her spending, started a small tutoring business after school, and opened a savings account. By the time she graduated, she had $3,000 saved for college.

Years later, she became a financial counselor; helping other families take control of their money just like she had. Lila's story is proof that financial education doesn't just change your wallet; it changes your life.

Reflection Questions:

1. What lessons from this book do you want to carry into your future?
2. What short, medium, and long-term goals do you want to set?
3. How can you make sure you keep learning about money as you grow?
4. What will your money story be?

Activities: Building Your Financial Future

1. Create Your 5-Year Financial Vision Board

Use paper, poster board, or a digital tool to design your vision for the next five years. Include images, drawings, or words that represent your goals (education, travel, savings, investments, acts of giving, or anything else that inspires you).

Label each goal with the year you'd like to achieve it and a short description of what steps you'll take to get there.

2. Write a Letter to Future You

On a separate piece of paper, write a letter to yourself five years from now. Describe where you hope to be financially and personally. Include the goals you're working toward, the habits you want to keep, and the lessons you don't want to forget.

Seal the letter in an envelope or store it in a safe place. Open it in five years to see how far you've come.

Closing Thought

Your financial future isn't written yet, it's something you build day by day. Every dollar you earn, save, invest, or give tells part of your story.

Final Assessment: Michelle's Budget Challenge

Introduction

In this capstone activity, you'll meet Michelle, a 24-year-old marketing coordinator living in Chicago. After graduating college a couple of years ago with a degree in Economics, she was able to land a job in the Chicago suburbs.

She earns a salary of $55,000 per year, but like many young professionals, she's struggling to manage her money. She is currently $40,000 in debt between student loans, a car loan, and credit card debt.

Your task is to analyze her current budget, identify problems, and recommend changes that can put her on the path to financial success.

This exercise will help you bring together everything you've learned about earning, managing, saving, investing, and giving. As you work through it, remember: the goal isn't perfection, it's awareness, action, and progress.

Michelle's Story

Michelle lives in a trendy neighborhood in the city where her one-bedroom studio apartment costs $1,700 per month. She enjoys city life; grabbing daily lattes, ordering takeout several times a week, and using rideshares to get around.

Although she works full-time, student loans, a car loan, and credit card debt are keeping her in the red each month. She feels like she's doing everything "right," but somehow, her bank account keeps shrinking.

She wants to learn how to fix her habits, pay down debt, and finally start saving for her future. Let's look at where her money is actually going.

Michelle's Current Monthly Budget

Category	Monthly Amount	Annual Amount
Take-home Pay	$3,600	$43,200
Rent	$1,700	$20,400
Utilities (Electric, Internet, etc.)	$200	$2,400
Groceries	$350	$4,200
Eating Out & Takeout	$300	$3,600
Coffee Shops	$120	$1,440
Transportation (Gas, Insurance, Rideshares)	$230	$2,760
Health Insurance & Medical	$200	$2,400
Subscriptions & Entertainment	$40	$480
Student Loan Payment	$250	$3,000
Credit Card Payment	$200	$2,400
Car Loan Payment	$300	$3,600
Miscellaneous Spending	$130	$1,560
Net Balance	**–$420**	**–$5,040**

Michelle's current budget leaves her short by about $420 each month. While she earns a solid income for her age, her lifestyle choices and debt payments are holding her back from saving or investing.

Each subsection will ask you to write down what her new budget line will be after your changes. You will plug these numbers in later to see how well you can balance her budget later.

Imagine yourself in Michelle's shoes, or imagine that she is someone you know well. If your recommendations make her life too miserable, you can and probably should leave a little more room in her budget. For example, she would save a lot of money by only eating rice and beans, but that may not be a realistic expectation for many people.

Category-by-Category Questions

Use the space below to evaluate each part of Michelle's budget. Identify what she's doing wrong, suggest changes, and estimate how much money she could save by making smarter choices.

Income

Michelle's sole source of income is her salary from her role as a Marketing Coordinator. Although this job pays pretty well given her age, it is not enough to cover her monthly budget and make progress on paying down her debt. While much of her troubles are due to out-of-control spending, she can speed up the process of getting out of debt and growing her net worth by increasing her income.

1. What can Michelle do to increase her salary? If she is able to get a promotion to the next level up (ex. Associate Marketing Manager), how much could she make?

Note: You can view salary ranges for job titles in specific job markets by using a tool like Glassdoor.

____

____

____

2. In addition to her marketing skills and knowledge of economics, Michelle has a passion for volleyball; a sport she played in high school. Are there any side hustles or entrepreneurial projects that Michelle could start to make

some extra money?

3. Are there any part time or gig jobs that Michelle could take in the short term while she pays off debt to bring in some extra money (ex. Uber, Instacart, etc.)?

4. How much extra money could Michelle earn each month with your suggested actions? How much money would her take home pay be now ($3,600 + extra money)?

Housing

With housing currently taking up over 47% ($1,700/$3,600) of her monthly post tax income, Michelle is living in an unaffordable apartment given her income. It is generally recommended to have your housing costs be 25%-33% of your take home pay, and she is well above that range.

Unless she can significantly increase her income, it will be necessary for her to move to a cheaper apartment and/or get a roommate.

Consider This: If she gets a roommate, she will be able to split utilities.

1. When Michelle got hired, she immediately found an apartment she liked in a high demand location that she always wanted to live in. Why was this the wrong decision?

____

____

____

2. Help Michelle find a more affordable housing option. Search online for apartments for rent and roommates wanted in the Chicago suburban market (within 25 miles of Niles, IL). Record prices and locations for three total options.

One option will be the nicest you can find within the 25%-33% range of the take home pay from the prior subsection, one will be the cheapest reasonable option, and the other will be priced in between.

Nicest Option:

____

____

Middle Option:

____

____

Budget Option:

____

____

3. Select one option, and record what her new monthly housing cost will be.

____

____

Utilities

Living alone, Michelle is covering the full cost of her utilities, including energy, internet, and her phone bill. Fortunately, her apartment complex covers gas and water, but the $200 in monthly utilities are still a large hole in her budget. As of now, her specific bills are:

Energy: $70

Internet: $60

Phone: $70

1. Are there cheaper providers or bundled plans available? Search online for deals on phone and internet plans, and record the best deal you find here:

____

____

____

2. Could she lower her energy bill by changing any habits?

____

____

____

3. Estimate how much monthly utilities would be with the phone and internet plans you selected added to her energy bill. If you believe you can save a few dollars on energy with the habits listed above, you can use $65 as the energy bill.

Food and Coffee

Between groceries ($350), restaurant food ($300), and coffee on the go ($120), Michelle is spending over $25 a day ($770 per month) on food and drinks. This amounts to over 21% of her take home pay.

Michelle appreciates the convenience of having her food made for her, and much of her grocery budget goes to frozen and prepared meals.

1. Should Michelle stop drinking coffee to save $120 a month? If not, how can she significantly lower this part of her budget? Note: her office has free coffee in the break room.

2. Buying groceries and cooking your own meals is often the best way to lower this part of your budget. Buying individual ingredients is often cheaper than buying a fully prepared meal in the frozen foods section.

Homemade meals can vary from cheap options like rice and beans ($1-$2 per meal) to cheaper versions of nice restaurant meals (ex. steak and potatoes could be $8-$10 depending on the cut).

If Michelle wants to spend as little as possible, she can live on rice and beans (with vegetables and seasonings mixed in) for roughly $2 per meal/$6 per day/$180 per month. However, she will probably want some variety and other nutrients.

What types of meals should Michelle be eating now that she is working to get out of debt and establish good financial habits? What would her monthly grocery expense be under this plan?

____

____

____

____

3. Should Michelle continue to go to restaurants and order take-out food? If yes, how often should she go, and what should her monthly budget be?

____

____

____

____

Transportation

Between car insurance, gas, and the occasional ride share, Michelle is spending $230 per month in this category. Her car is a ten-year-old sedan that she bought used (Hyundai Sonata). Her specific costs are:

Insurance (most basic coverage): $125

Gas: $80

Rideshares: $25

1. Car insurance prices can vary greatly by company and term. In general, you can get discounts when you pay for several months at a time. Finding companies that spend less on marketing and are able to provide a deeper discount is smart as well.

Look for some car insurance quotes for a car like Michelle's. Can you find a better deal? How much would she pay per month under this plan?

____

____

____

2. Gas prices are largely out of our control, though some local gas stations may be consistently 10 cents per gallon cheaper than nearby stations. The best way to lower this cost is to limit how much you drive. This can include walking more, biking places, using public transportation, or carpooling.

Michelle could save 1-2 gallons worth of gas by walking or biking to places she currently takes short drives to. She also has a couple of coworkers who live nearby.

How can Michelle save money on her monthly gas expense? How much money would she spend on gas each month if she followed your recommendations?

____

____

____

____

____

3. Michelle occasionally takes a rideshare service (ex. Uber, Lyft) to get to a place in the city where parking would be more expensive. She could save money by meeting up with her friends first, then splitting the cost, but she usually goes alone for convenience.

Do you think that she should save some money on this expense by pooling with friends? Should she stop going places that she would need a ride share service for altogether? How much money would she spend on ride shares each month if she followed your recommendations?

____

____

____

____

____

Debt Payments

Michelle's current debt payments total $750 per month. See below for the minimum monthly payment, as well as the interest rate and remaining balance of each:

Student loan: $250; 6.5% interest, $25,000 remaining balance

Car loan: $300; 7.5% interest; $6,000 remaining balance

Credit Card: $200; 20% interest; $9,000 remaining balance

1. Which debts have the highest interest rates?

____

____

____

2. Would you recommend for her to take the debt snowball method (lowest balance first), or the credit avalanche method (highest interest rate first)? Why?

____

____

____

____

3. Revisit this section after you fill in Michelle's updated budget. The budget surplus you create will be used to pay off debt and put her in a position where this section of her budget will be used on saving/investing when she is debt free.

How much money can she spend each month on debt payments on her new budget?

Entertainment, Subscriptions, & Miscellaneous Spending

Michelle thinks she is saving money by cutting the cord; subscribing to individual services rather than paying for the monthly cable bundle. See below for her subscriptions and monthly usage.

Netflix (Premium): $25 (45 hours)

Disney+: $10 (15 hours)

Discovery+: $5 (10 hours)

She also spends $130 a month on additional entertainment and miscellaneous expenses. These include household expenses (tissues, shampoo, etc.), paying for a night out (ex. bowling), and more.

1. Which subscriptions could she pause or cancel? Are there cheaper subscriptions that she can get to watch the same shows? Explain your reasoning and record how much her monthly subscriptions will cost now.

2. Are there free alternatives for movies, music, or social activities? What activities should she do in place of more expensive ones from time to time?

3. What tools could help her stay mindful of her money day-to-day?

Michelle's Smart Budget (After Changes)

Enter your amounts from the prior sections in the table below.

Category	Monthly Amount	Annual Amount
Take-home Pay	$	$
Rent	$	$
Utilities	$	$
Groceries	$	$
Eating Out	$	$
Coffee Shops	$	$
Transportation	$	$
Health Insurance & Medical	$	$
Subscriptions & Entertainment	$	$
Student Loan Payment	$	$
Credit Card Payment	$	$
Car Loan Payment	$	$
Roth IRA Contribution	$	$
Emergency Fund Savings	$	$
Net Balance	**$**	**$**

By increasing her income and lowering costs, her monthly budget has gone from being down $420 to now bringing in more money than she spends. Now, take the monthly net balance and apply it to her debt.

Calculate how long it will take for her to pay off each debt. Keep in mind that when one debt is paid off, the minimum payment for that loan can now be added to your monthly payment on the next debt.

Once her debts are gone, she can redirect that same money toward her emergency fund, investments, and/or long-term goals.

Becoming debt-free not only improves her cash flow, but also reduces stress and gives her the flexibility to invest more aggressively in her future.

Learning Moment: 401(k) and Roth IRA

A **401(k)** is an employer-sponsored retirement account that allows you to contribute pre-tax income. This lowers your taxable income today while helping you save for retirement. Many employers offer matching contributions (essentially free money) so Michelle should check whether her company provides a match and aim to contribute enough to receive the full benefit.

A **Roth IRA** is a retirement account you fund with after-tax income. The money grows tax-free, and you can withdraw it tax-free in retirement. Since Michelle is young and likely in a lower tax bracket now than she will be later, the Roth IRA offers long-term advantages. Even a $100 monthly contribution can grow significantly over time.

Starting both early gives her a powerful head start on her future wealth. Investing consistently (even in small amounts) can have an enormous impact over decades. If she is able to start maxing out her annual contributions to her Roth IRA once she is debt free in her 20's, she will almost certainly be a millionaire by the time she retires.

Reflection Questions

- What specific changes made the biggest difference in Michelle's budget?
- Which changes would be most realistic for your own life?
- How can understanding tax-advantaged accounts help you grow your future wealth?
- How would being debt-free change Michelle's life in five years?

Closing Thought

Michelle's story shows that financial stability doesn't just come from earning more; it comes from managing what you already have wisely. Every dollar counts, and every decision shapes your financial future.

Now it's your turn. Build your plan, run your numbers, and start taking charge of your money story today.

Final Reflection:

Future You Reflection:
Write 2-3 short paragraphs describing how you'll apply what you've learned to your own finances. What habits, decisions, or tools will you start using to build your own financial future?

Afterword

Thank you for joining us on this journey through *Mastering Money*. Over these pages, you have explored how money really works; how it is earned, managed, spent, saved, and invested. You have seen how small daily choices can add up to big long-term results, and how confidence grows each time you take charge of your finances instead of letting them control you.

You may have discovered that managing money is not just about numbers, but about priorities. You may have realized that budgeting brings freedom, not restriction. You may have seen how debt can weigh you down, but also how discipline and planning can lift you back up. Along the way, you practiced setting goals, solving real-world challenges, and thinking like an investor in your own future.

Whether you worked through this book independently, as part of your homeschooling, or alongside your family, we hope it gave you tools that will serve you for years to come. Parents, you may have found that you learned something new right beside your kids, and that is part of what makes **Life Skills Lab** special. Each lesson in this series is designed to help families grow together, building the knowledge and confidence that make adult life easier and more meaningful.

Life Skills Lab is a growing series of practical workbooks that teach essential and often overlooked real-world skills that many adults say they never learned in school. Each book blends stories, activities, and reflection to turn complex ideas into simple, engaging lessons you can actually use. From giving and gratitude to entrepreneurship, smart shopping, and media literacy, every title in the series focuses on helping young people develop the character and confidence they will need to thrive.

These books are written by a husband-and-wife team with their own children in mind. These are lessons we want them to learn early so they can thrive, make wise choices, and build lives of purpose, generosity, and success. *Mastering Money* is one of the most in-depth books in the series, but others expand on the topics you have started here and introduce new skills you will use throughout your life.

At Good Buddy Books, our mission is to create resources that spark connection, learning, and growth for kids and families. We would love to hear from you. What budgeting strategy helped you most? Which activity changed the way you think about money? What financial goal are you most excited to reach?

You can share your reflections with us anytime at **goodbuddybooks.com**, where you will also find updates on the **Life Skills Lab** series and other titles designed to inspire your journey.

Thank you for letting us be part of your learning, your family time, and your growth. We believe that every smart financial decision, no matter how small, brings you one step closer to freedom, generosity, and confidence.

We cannot wait to see what you will do with the skills you have learned here.

Until next time,

—The Life Skills Lab Team

Keep the Learning Going!

We hope you've had a great time with ***Mastering Money***! The learning and personal growth doesn't have to stop here. If you've enjoyed learning new skills and making an impact with this book, there's a growing world of **Life Skills Lab** waiting for you.

Discover More Good Buddy Books

Want to explore our full collection of books, get sneak peeks of upcoming titles, or just learn more about what we do? Visit our website!

www.goodbuddybooks.com

Find the Entire Life Skills Lab Series on Amazon

This is just the beginning of your journey! The ***Life Skills Lab*** series will continue with more books designed to help kids and teens grow into confident, capable adults. Find updates at goodbuddybooks.com, and look for Life Skills Lab titles on Amazon.

Life Skills Lab Series Page on Amazon

Made in United States
North Haven, CT
05 November 2026

21765509R00098